The *art* *of*
TURNED
BOWLS

The *art* of
TURNED
BOWLS

Designing Bowls with
a World-Class Turner

RICHARD
RAFFAN

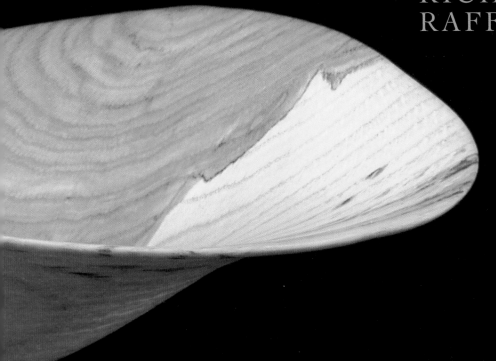

The Taunton Press

The Taunton Press
Inspiration for hands-on living®

The Taunton Press, Inc., 63 South Main Street, PO Box 5506, Newtown, CT 06470-5506
e-mail: tp@taunton.com

Editor: Rick Mastelli
Cover Designer: Amy Russo
Interior Designer: Susan Fazekas
Layout Artist: Deborah Fillion
Photographer: Richard Raffan, except where noted
Illustrator: Lee Hochgraf
Production: Image & Word, Montpelier, VT

Library of Congress Cataloging-in-Publication Data
Raffan, Richard.
  The art of turned bowls : designing bowls with a world-class turner / Richard Raffan.
     p. cm.
  Includes bibliographical references and index.
  ISBN 978-1-56158-954-8 (alk. paper)
  1. Turning. 2. Bowls (Tableware) I. Title.
  TT201.R32 2008
  684'.083--dc22   2008019676

Printed in the United States of America
10 9 8 7 6 5 4 3 2 1

The following manufacturers/names appearing in *The Art of Turned Bowls* are
trademarks: Arbortech Woodcarver; Dremel; Nylox; Robert Sorby; Teknatool/Nova

ABOUT YOUR SAFETY

Working with wood is inherently dangerous. Using hand or power tools improperly
or ignoring safety practices can lead to permanent injury or even death. Don't try to
perform operations you learn about here (or elsewhere) unless you're certain they
are safe for you. If something about an operation doesn't feel right, don't do it. Look
for another way. We want you to enjoy the craft, so please keep safety foremost in
your mind whenever you're in the shop.

ACKNOWLEDGMENTS

THIS BOOK IS ABOUT FORM AND WHAT YOU CAN DO WITH IT. I am interested in very simple, even stark, forms and rarely consider my forays into embellishments successful enough to be seen outside my workshop. So rather than foist my less-than-satisfactory efforts on an unsuspecting reader, I approached turners whose work I admire, inviting them to share their creations and ideas. We aim to ignite some spark that inflames your creativity, and hope that you will resist the temptation to copy any particular bowl directly. Rather, you should take a good long look at the bowls that attract you, then ponder the ideas, textures, techniques, and so on, before shutting the book and setting out on your own path of discovery.

The Contributors

BENOÎT AVERLY is a full-time studio and production turner working in Saint Point, France. www.benoitaverly.com

TERRY BAKER trained as an industrial arts teacher majoring in ceramics. For 25 years he has been a full-time studio woodturner and artist working near Woy Woy, NSW, Australia.

DOUGLAS BELL, now teaching woodturning and design in Adelaide, Australia, is a retired architect and industrial designer.

LUKE CROWSEN of Papatoetoe, Auckland, New Zealand was fourteen when he turned his "Four-in-One" bowl.

LIAM FLYNN is a full-time studio turner. He lives and works in County Limerick, Ireland, where his family have been joiners and woodworkers for generations. www.liamflynn.com

ANDREW GITTOES is a full-time production and studio woodturner in Goulburn, NSW, Australia.

ART LIESTMAN is Professor of Computing Science at Simon Fraser University, Vancouver, Canada. He began woodturning to make parts for an automated programmable xylophone, and intends to be a full-time studio turner upon retirement. www.artliestman.com

BILL LUCE, is a full-time studio woodturner living in Renton, WA, USA. www.billluce.com

FRED MORTON, living in Canberra, Australia, is an automotive mechanical engineer with a transmission repair business and more lathes than he needs.

PASCAL OUDET is an electronics engineer living in Goncelin, France. He writes about and demonstrates all manner of turning techniques in both French and English. www.lavieenbois.com

GORDON PEMBRIDGE was raised in Kenya until the age of ten, when his family moved to New Zealand. He worked in the photographic trade for twenty years before becoming a self-employed graphic designer/fine artist involved with illustration, photography, photographic restoration, fine art commissions, and now woodturning. He lives in Auckland, New Zealand.

ANDREW POTOCNIK, Macleod West, Victoria, Australia, has worked wood since his childhood. An industrial arts teacher, he also writes for *Australian Wood Review* and, as an artist-in-wood, exhibits regularly.

VAUGHN RICHMOND is a former automotive mechanical engineer, now a full-time studio turner who also writes, lectures, and teaches design workshops. He is based in Warwick, Western Australia.

LIZ AND NEIL SCOBIE were trained to teach textiles and design, and industrial arts, respectively. Liz is now a textile artist, Neil a cabinetmaker who also turns wood. They live near Coffs Harbour, NSW, Australia, where they run courses and make a range of furniture and textile art.

MIKE SCOTT has lived as a maker of wooden vessels and a sculptor for the past twenty years. He worked previously as an accountant before dropping out to study Eastern philosophy, after which he took a degree in creative arts. He is based in Llanddeusant, Anglesea, UK. www.chaiwood.com

TERRY SCOTT is a builder and property developer in Papakura, Auckland, New Zealand. He reckons he turns at least eight hours a week.

TIM SKILTON became a full-time woodturner seventeen years ago after a career in the mining and construction industries. By then he had developed the Skilton sanders, power-sanding pads, and abrasive disks which he manufactures in Adelaide, South Australia, and exports worldwide.

Additional contributors, represented by bowls I admire and have in my bowl collection, include Al Gruntwagin, Jim Partridge, Michael Peterson, Dale Nish, Rude Osolnik, and Vic Wood.

My thanks also to those who helped me get a better idea of where turners source their wood at the beginning of the twenty-first century. To this end, I emailed woodturning buddies and former students around the world. The following, in no particular order, were kind enough to respond:

Peter Filmer, Mark Leech, Ray Key, Peter Hughes, Ciarán Forbes, Ray Lanham, John Cobb, Rod Tier, Mike Mahoney, Andi Wolfe, Michael O'Donnell, Dave Regester, Rusty Harrison, Dennis Liggett, Bill Bowers, Larry Genender, Roger Dunn, Lyle Jamieson, Dale Larson, Dennis Gooding, Bonnie Klein, Robin Bryan, Michael Werner, David Hammond, Andy Barnum, Ruth Niles, Keith Gotschall, J. Paul Fennel, Mike Sublett, Terry Martin, Angelo Iafrate, Peter Bloomfield, Dick Sing, Bill Shean, and Dick Vietch, who did a survey of three woodturning clubs in Auckland, New Zealand, and then collated ninety-six replies. Their input is reflected in Chapter 2.

And finally my most sincere thanks to Rick Mastelli for another enjoyable editing experience. Without his prompting, insights, and hawk-like eye for detail, this would be a much poorer book.

Contents

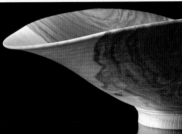

Fumed oak pot
by Liam Flynn.

INTRODUCTION

M Y DICTIONARIES DEFINE A BOWL generally as a nearly hemispherical vessel, whose width is greater than its height, used to contain liquids or foods. This implies forms that are open rather than enclosed, so, for this book, I've broadened my terms of reference to include enclosed forms that are similarly wider than their height, but with a rim diameter as small as one third the diameter of the bowl.

It is clear, browsing woodturning websites and exhibitions, that bowls continue to be a favorite project for turners of all skill levels, still outnumbering hollow forms and vessels as well as spindle work. I believe this is because an open bowl is an ideal form for displaying spectacular grain and because bowl turners like making shavings. It is easy to create a bowl that, by virtue of its rich color and/or wild grain patterns or thinness, will draw gasps of admiration. Any beginner can achieve this within an hour or two, given a flashy bit of wood, a range of abrasives, and some finish to gloss-up the wood and bring out the color. What is not so easy is creating a bowl that feels nicely balanced in your hands when you pick it up, and that would still look good if painted black. The bright colors of freshly cut and finished wood soon begin to fade and mellow, ending up dark or golden brown.

Consequently, it pays to attend to the form and the tactile qualities of a bowl because, eventually, that's all you've got.

Despite the obvious care and attention that has gone into creating most of the bowls I see in craft shows and galleries, the majority remain somewhat cumbersome, even clunky, to the eye as well as the hand, even when turned thin. So often it's a case of so near yet so far, when a small adjustment to the profile or inner curve would have yielded an infinitely better form. Having said that, it is a fact that most of the bowls I look at now are light-years ahead of what was on show at woodturning symposiums in the early 1980s when the few good bowls stood out from a morass that were mediocre to bad. Then, critiques comparing good, bad, and downright ugly versions of the same basic shape, often from the same turner, were a key symposium activity that set people thinking about design. Constructive comments helped turners become more aware of what goes into creating a well-proportioned bowl and what constitutes a flowing curve or a good finish. The turned bowls we see today are the result of those sessions. Concurrently, improved chucks and techniques and a considerable amount of supporting literature, videos, DVDs, and now the Internet, have enabled turners to implement their designs with greater confidence, allowing them to concentrate more on what they are turning, rather than how.

Often we find it difficult to quantify why one bowl seems better than another, and the main purpose of this book is to provide points for consideration. Is it the difference between a curve that flows and one that doesn't? Or is it the visual impact of the size of a base? It helps to compare similar or near identical bowls, identifying exactly why one looks and feels better than another.

When assessing bowls with groups of students, I like to select three that are similar, preferably by the same person (to eliminate bruised egos). It is immaterial how good or bad the bowls are. All I need is to pick one as a benchmark; then I can point out all the negative features of the lesser of the three, and why one is better than the other. I take the view that there is always room for improvement in everything, even though that might be barely perceptible.

If you are serious about creating better bowls, turn a number of similar bowls using bland wood, then select the best and use that as the model for another set. Every now and again, cut a few in half to ascertain more thoroughly where the differences lie, and what makes the ones you prefer better than the others.

If a bowl is to survive, it has to be of a quality that will encourage its current owner to keep it safe. The form has to be good. In general, ill-conceived objects do not survive generations except as curios, whereas anything well designed stands a better chance. Many medieval bowls handed down to us are patched or sewn together; you don't bother doing that unless the object is special. There would have been plenty of less attractive but equally functional bowls available to replace those damaged.

The critiques of the mid-1980s were so successful that by 1990 it was difficult to find a bad bowl at an event like the annual Utah Symposium Instant Gallery. However, in recent years, after making a few dozen bowls, turners are often keen to "move beyond the round and brown," without having created a really satisfactory bowl. The pressure is on to enhance and embellish bowls. So now we have a lot of round and brown bowls with paint, feathers, beads, burn marks, and just about anything that can be attached to wood or penetrate it. Often carving distorts the form so much that any association with a lathe all but vanishes. Much of this is work striving to be Art with a capital A, but being different doesn't automatically qualify something as art. Your bowl might be unique, being stained with the blood of virgin roosters (for depth of color) and adorned with the milk-teeth of Pomeranian dwarves set in a frieze of 24-carat gold. It might be extremely well made of expensive materials, and although of hideous design, might still appeal to those impressed by novelty, kitsch, or extravagance. It may make your work collectible, but being different is rarely a passport to good design. No matter what you do to a bowl by way of embellishment, the basic form will always manifest itself through the frippery.

Style and Originality

A personal style develops unless rigorously controlled. Even in a world where everything seems to have been done before, it is still possible to make objects that stand out in a crowd. To create anything that is easily identifiable as yours, all you have to do is let your own sense of balance and proportion, along with your own quirky way of doing things, come through into your work. Each of us has differing ways of interpreting measurements and tolerances, and we work with wood that is not a stable medium. Hand-turned bowls that look identical across a room rarely are when you get to handle them. Whether the world at large will judge your efforts as something we should aspire to will be another matter. But if you need to sell your work, it's good to know that there are enough people somewhere who consider what you do to be wonderful and are prepared to purchase it—even at ridiculously high prices. All you have to do is find them.

This book describes my approach to designing bowls. There is virtually no technical information on cutting and turning techniques, as these are dealt with in detail in my books *Turning Bowls*, *Turning Wood*, and *Taunton's Complete Guide to Turning* (all published by The Taunton Press, Newtown, CT). I offer basic information on decorative techniques. For further information on different ways of achieving the various effects, I refer you to the numerous books and magazine articles available, as well as the Internet.

Inspirational Sources

It is our good fortune that a vast quantity of inspirational material from all over the world is available in museums, books, magazines, and now the Internet. Look at as much as you can, and particularly at what has been done by previous generations in all manner of craft disciplines. Traditional potters, basket weavers, and glass and metal workers have worked and reworked most bowl forms for millennia. These generations of artisans have weeded out the less successful forms, and those that survive surely must be the crème de la crème. You don't have to reinvent the wheel to find a good form. Having picked out the ideas and objects that appeal, go away and implement them without visual reference. Your own version will emerge, manifestly yours, soon enough. And from that might even emerge a genre and then a tradition.

A set of techniques that enables you to execute your ideas with confidence comes about only through lots of repetition. Try to forget about catering to a market or impressing your relatives or critics. Create for yourself, and as your freed spirit emerges, your work will improve.

The inspirational sources that influence my bowls are many and varied. When I began turning wood in England in 1970, I joined the Devon Guild of Craftsmen where I was fortunate to learn quite a bit about form and function from several renowned potters working within Japanese traditions. The influence of Japanese and Korean ceramics on my bowls is obvious, but I feel that I'm also working within the traditions of the nineteenth-century Appalachian, Shaker, and British bowl turners who created wonderful, simple, open, practical bowls for domestic use.

My forte, and indeed my keenest interest and on-going challenge, is in creating visually strong, simple forms. Constantly in the back of my mind is Mies van der Rohe's aphorism "less is more," although I aspire to the more demanding Japanese "more with less." Simple bowls are definitely out of fashion in high-end galleries as I write, the majority of turners and collectors seeming to feel that there's nothing to making simple bowls, and that such bowls are always inconsequential. Of course simple is rarely as simple as it looks, and looking tells only half the story: to appreciate a bowl fully you need to handle it so you can feel the balance, the wall thickness, and the texture of the surfaces. This is what makes a good bowl such a delight to use day to day.

One of the joys of turning bowls is playing with form, with curves in all their different manifestations. We see and feel curves in profiles, across surfaces, ever subtle, ever varying. But we can assess whether a curve or form is successful or beautiful only in relation to other similar forms. So much of what we create is not quite right, a just miss. A curve is just too full here, a line too low there, the proportions vaguely unsettling but for not readily discernible reasons. Then once we begin combining elements, it is enormously difficult to bring all the elements together into a truly satisfying whole.

For myself, the creation of visually strong, simple forms remains one of life's great challenges, and the search for those is basically what this book is all about.

—1—

WOOD

What to Look For and
Where to Find It

ON THIS EARTH MORE THAN A thousand species of trees and many sizeable woody shrubs are available for turning. Trees, and the woods they yield, are classified broadly as hardwoods or softwoods, categorized not by the density of the wood but by how they reproduce. Most woodworkers are more concerned with a wood's working qualities, its fitness for a given purpose, and what it looks like when polished. If it cuts cleanly and looks good, we're not too fussed whether it's a hardwood or softwood, although it's nice to know.

Essentially, hardwoods do not have seed cones, whereas softwoods do. In addition, hardwoods have vessels, known as pores, that are absent in softwoods. These holes can be seen on cleanly sliced end grain using a simple 10× hand lens. Hardwoods such as ash, cherry, or walnut are more likely to be of interest to bowl turners because these are usually stronger, denser, and less likely than softwoods to dent if knocked. Hardwood end grain is usually easier to cut cleanly—and you have *that* to deal with in four sections of every bowl. There are exceptions, however, like balsa, whose low density makes it ideal for model aircraft—but not much good for a salad bowl. And there are hard softwoods,

such as yew and juniper, that are wonderful for bowl turning.

Plenty of books have been written about wood, its properties and uses, and you should refer to these for information regarding specific woods. From the woodworking magazines, also full of wood lore, you soon learn what turners favor. Just keep in mind, as you read, that every rule has exceptions. Some of my best and worst experiences at the lathe have been with what appeared to be almost identical

▲ To achieve such a smooth profile on a softwood like this Douglas fir, the wood has to be cut, not sanded. Heavy sanding would etch away the soft wood between the hard growth rings. The inside of this natural-edge bowl made by Bill Luce is sandblasted.

◄ Beneath the thick bark of many burls is a spiky surface. Sandblasted, this surface was retained for a wide rim on the bowl pictured at the bottom of page 20.

13

CONVERTING A LOG
TO BOWL BLANKS

The stability of a board is related to the alignment of the grain within it. The board that's least likely to warp during seasoning will be quartersawn, as at **A**, where the growth rings on the end grain lie roughly perpendicular to the wide faces of the board and parallel to the sides. A quartersawn board should remain flat as it dries; shrinkage in width will be moderate. In a flatsawn board, **B**, where the growth rings lie closer to parallel to the faces, the board will cup away from the heart as it dries. If the heart, or pith, of the log is off-center in a flatsawn board, as at **C**, the board will warp unevenly. In all cases the grain along the length of the log should run across a bowl, parallel to the base and rim.

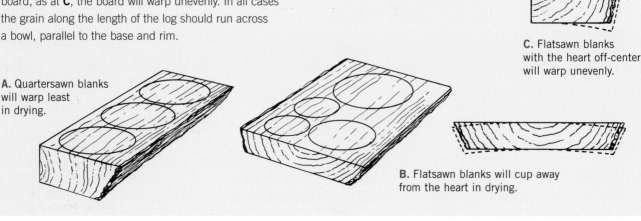

C. Flatsawn blanks with the heart off-center will warp unevenly.

A. Quartersawn blanks will warp least in drying.

B. Flatsawn blanks will cup away from the heart in drying.

samples of the same species. Most Burmese teak, for example, is a forgiving material, a pleasure to work, easy to cut, sand, and finish. But I have encountered boards so hard that I never switched off the grinder, my tools dulled so quickly. Fortunately, it is usually possible to detect the likelihood of such problems in advance, so before discussing where you can find your raw material, let's consider what to look for when assessing a log or board. It also helps to know a bit about wood in general, where its strength lies, and how it reacts during seasoning.

In a perfect world logs would remain stable as they season. They might shrink a bit, but never split, and you could cut up wood as you might a lump of cheese or clay. A very few woods, like teak and mahogany, approach this ideal, but most of the woods you'll encounter will warp, twist, and check before they reach equilibrium.

The grain of all wood lies more or less parallel to the tree's pith, flowing up the trunk and out into the branches. A tree is little more than a bundle of fibers built up annually to create the growth rings seen on the end of every log or board. Around the bundle is bark. The length of the fibers gives wood tremendous longitudinal strength; whereas if you take a thin slice off the end of a log or board, you'll find it easy to break or even punch through. For this reason, the grain is best aligned across a bowl, parallel to the base. Grain aligned perpendicular to the base gives you short grain in the base that, if thin, would be unable to withstand any sort of impact. The thin walls are also very weak and likely to split with the slightest knock. Grain alignment is very important, and not only for the structural integrity of your bowl. End grain is particularly arduous to hollow,

▲ While solid enough, this 14-in. (355mm) log is too split to consider for large bowls. Severe splitting on the outside and radial splits from the pith mean that defect-free blanks will be smaller than 6 in. by 2 in. (150mm × 50mm).

▲ Wood darkens with age. Turned in 1980, the Jim Partridge holly bowl (top) has yellowed from white; the yew (left) started bright orange; the osage orange (right) darkened from very bright yellowy orange.

whereas blanks with grain running parallel to the bowl's base are much easier to work.

This means that whenever you're looking at a log or even a chunk of wood for bowls, you think in terms of cutting very short boards with the grain running parallel to the faces and sides. Some boards will be only slightly longer than the disk to be sawn from them, so you must make allowances for any small splits on the end grain that are likely to develop and will have to be removed.

The stability of a board is related to the alignment of the grain within it, as shown in the drawing on the facing page. As soon as a tree is felled, it begins to dry. Newly felled logs are very wet, so they can shrink dramatically as they dry. But shrinkage is mainly tangential and radial to the growth rings. Longitudinal shrinkage, that is, along the length of a log, is negligible. Typically small splits, beginning on the crosscut surface of a log and radiating from the pith, appear soon after it is felled. Then, as the sapwood begins to dry and shrink, the outside of the log also begins to split, pulled apart by tangential forces. A good strategy to alleviate this is to split a log in two along any major crack. It is also good practice to rough-turn your logs into bowls as soon as you can, before the wood starts splitting. The roughed bowls will warp (you finish-turn them after they have seasoned), but splitting should be minimal, and you will get a lot more from each log than if you leave it solid. For detailed instruction on twice-turning bowls, see my book *Turning Bowls* (The Taunton Press, 2002).

What to Look For

When assessing any log or board, you should be on the lookout for several things—some good, some very undesirable. Let's start with what you should avoid, because wood that is a mass of cracks, rot, and insect holes, or laced with fencing wire is a waste of time and effort, no matter how good the color or grain. After that, you'll see how to seek out the better logs. Buying wood is usually a matter of eliminating poor choices, until you finally get to the this-is-better-than-that stage. Always remember that the bright colors of freshly sawn wood will fade, although strong grain patterns remain.

Splits and Cracks

Most logs and seasoned wood will have splits and cracks (known also as shakes or checks). For your own safety, you should never cut or use blanks with major splits running across a face. Cracked or split blanks spinning on a lathe can fly apart and cause serious injury, so split wood is always worth avoiding. Small surface checks are not dangerous. When you appraise a log or board, consider how you can cut blanks free of splits.

End-grain cracking is responsible for a lot of waste and must be cut away to reveal solid wood. Usually splits are obvious on the end of a log or board, but they can be very difficult to see as they peter out into solid wood. Always assume that you'll have to cut away at least 2 in. (50mm) beyond the discernable end of a split.

When examining end grain, look for ring shakes (also called cup shakes) that follow growth rings. In the photo at left the upper split between light sapwood and darker heart is large, and the growth-ring separation is obvious. The lower splits beneath the rot are more typical hairline splits. These usually run much deeper than end-grain cracks and often the length of a log. The fact that they follow growth rings makes them difficult to work around when you're cutting wide boards and blocks. I avoid any wood with ring shakes, as in my experience where there is one ring shake, there are more I can't see.

If you find longitudinal splits on or below the bark, ensure that there is enough solid wood between each for the thickness you require or that you can use the material for

▲ Ring shakes (also called cup shakes) are splits where growth rings have separated, here bordering pockets of early stages of rot. This log is a non-starter for bowls.

▶ The dark lines of incipient rot included a pipe of pulpy fibers. Note also borer holes on the lines of rot. Both areas were discarded when this oak was squared up for a blank.

▲ Small holes in a sawn board, often in the sapwood, indicate insect activity and consequent damage. There is no guarantee that the insects are gone (the small pile of powdery frass here suggests otherwise), and such wood is best avoided and removed from the proximity of seasoning boards.

other projects. Remember that longitudinal splits on the bark go towards the pith, so the thickness of a blank will be dictated by the inner distance between two splits, not by the distance immediately under the bark.

Rot and Decay

If you are looking at freshly felled logs from urban trees, chances are they will have some rot or decay. Urban trees are rarely felled in their prime. Rot begins when water seeps into the tree through a split crotch or some other damage. In the photo at lower left on the facing page the dark blotches on the end grain are incipient rot, and the soft spot in the middle is a rotten pipe that follows the grain through the block.

Trees can also die of disease or through insect attack. Each spells the beginning of a slow death for a tree, and one will often follow the other. Once a tree starts decaying, borers and termites move in and begin recycling the wood back into the earth. In the photo at lower right on the facing page several small black borer holes dot the lines of incipient rot that creates the lines of darker grain on the long-grain face. You need to check for insects so you don't carry them back to your workshop or wood pile. Some insects live only in the sapwood, rarely wandering off into the heartwood. When examining boards, look for holes in the bark and on sawn surfaces. These can be small and difficult to see. If you are looking at stacks of seasoned boards, check for small piles of powder-fine dust or frass that indicate insect activity.

If borers have been active enough, their holes can become a feature in themselves, as shown in Dale Nish's "Wormy Ash Bowl" at right.

If you are looking at freshly felled logs from urban trees, chances are they will have some rot or decay.

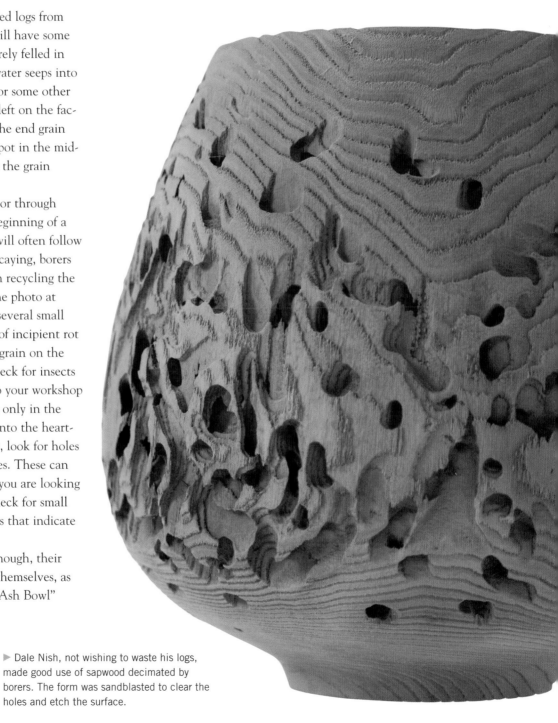

▶ Dale Nish, not wishing to waste his logs, made good use of sapwood decimated by borers. The form was sandblasted to clear the holes and etch the surface.

▼ ▶ Spalting is incipient rot, but if you can catch it before the wood softens, the intricate webs of fine black lines look spectacular in a bowl.

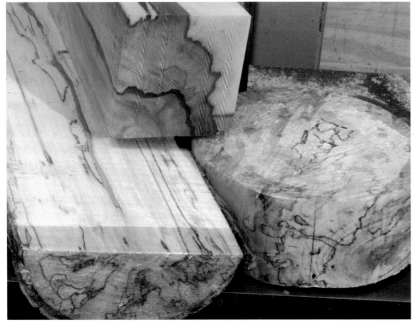

▶ In this quarter casuarina log, the rays radiate from the corner in the foreground. Any surface cut parallel to a ray will reveal wide ribbons or flecks of ultra-smooth grain like those visible here on the smooth face. The pink on the corner is a mineral deposit, like a thin layer of stone.

A tree in the early stages of fungal decay can offer some spectacular wood as it becomes stained or spalted. Spalting, being part of a rotting process, will often be associated with soft areas. If you can press your fingernail into such an area, the wood is not worth bothering with. But if you can catch it before the wood becomes too soft, you can find wonderfully intricate webs of fine black lines that are spectacular on a bowl. As with wine, wood is sometimes best just before it's no good.

Spalting is a fungal growth that is not healthy to breathe. When working with spalted wood you should ensure that the spores don't get into your lungs by wearing a respirator and using a good dust-extraction system.

Mineral and Metal Intrusions

In elms, casuarinas, maples, and several tropical hardwoods, I have often encountered seams of a mineral deposit that takes the edge off any tool. The casuarina log pictured at bottom left has a seam of pink stone-like deposit through the pith, seen on the corner in the center. On maples these more often appear as small grey patches surrounded by a greenish tinge, or a hard white film on a crack.

Where there are people, metal usually ends up in wood in the form of nails, staples, wire, or gun shot. Iron usually stains the surrounding wood black or blue/black, so such stains are a warning. Always check bark for nails. If you are using a lot of urban trees, a metal detector is a good investment. Big nails can ruin a sawblade.

Grain and Color

While this is a book about form and design, what attracts most people to most bowls initially is the grain in the wood and the color. Beyond a particular wood's structural and working properties, it is the infinite variety of grain patterns and rich and varying colors that make some woods so much more attractive and desirable than others. However, when you look at a weathering log or a seasoned board, neither grain nor color is immediately apparent.

To discover the color of a seasoned board, you'll need to plane the surface, but that will be a guide only as to what lies immediately beneath that surface. To get an idea of what's going on deep inside, you need to look at the freshly cut end grain. On seasoned or weathered wood, cut back the end grain a finger's thickness to get behind the darkened or silvery surface. Once the end grain is exposed, you'll see the thickness of the sap and any color variations in the heartwood. As is evident in the cut logs shown above right, the variations usually run the length of the material, although it's prudent to look at the other end for confirmation, particularly on sawn stock.

Remember that colors are at their most vibrant in freshly felled timber. As the wood dries, the colors fade to deep golds, browns, and near black. In some species the process takes years, in others a few weeks. In the long

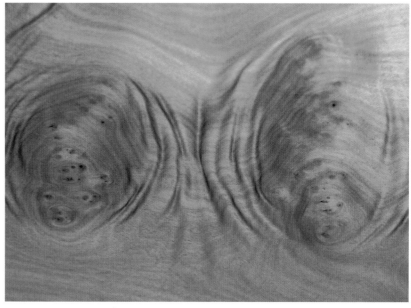

▲ Quilting figure around some knotted Tasmanian musk.

run, strong color variations will bring a richness to the wood as it is polished or takes on the patina imparted by life.

Figure

Some of the most interesting wild grain and figure come from the most stressed parts of a tree. Around crotches, burls, buttresses, and knots, you'll usually find highly figured wood. Wood from these sections is more likely to distort and split as it dries. The results, however, can be visually spectacular, so it's worth the risk.

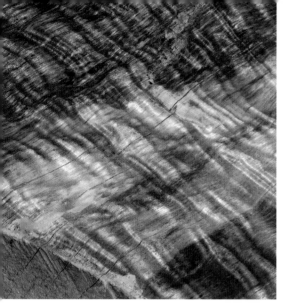

◀◀ Fiddleback ripples on a large red gum log (far left). The splits show that this wood needs to be rough-turned or sawn into small sections before degrading further. The shimmer of fiddleback figure, clearly seen in sanded areas, can be difficult to spot on rough-sawn surfaces of boards and turning blanks (left).

▶ On the end of this oak log, darker rings winding along the edges of the lighter growth rings indicate this log has spectacular figure. The bowl was cut from the other half of the log. Any surface cut parallel to the silver lines (rays) radiating from the pith will reveal the classic ribbon figure associated with quartersawn oak.

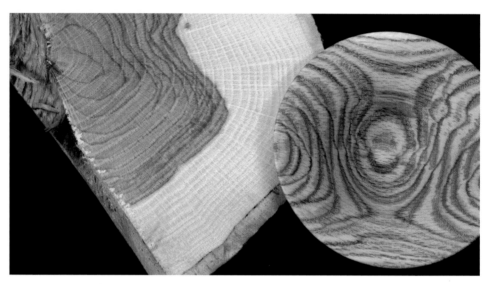

▼ Beneath the thick bark of many burls is a spiky surface. For the wide rim of this mallee burl bowl, the surface was sandblasted.

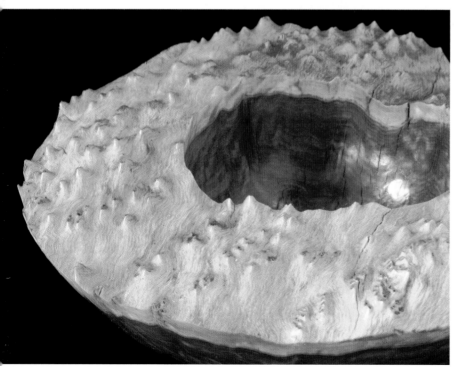

Corrugated fiddleback figure, seen in the photo at top left, is typically easy to spot on a log but more difficult to see on a sawn board. In the photo at top right the figure is evident in the sanded areas; on the rougher surfaces it can be confused with saw marks.

Strong rays (sometimes called medullary rays) show on end grain as radial lines like those on top of the log in the photo at the bottom of page 18 and in the photo above. These can be used to dramatic effect. Any surface cut parallel to these radial lines will reveal wide ribbons or flecks of ultra-smooth grain. Woods like oaks, London plane (or sycamore—depending on which side of the Atlantic you are), grevilleas, and many woods known as lacewood can be quartersawn to

While this is a book about form and design, what attracts most people to most bowls initially is the grain in the wood and the color.

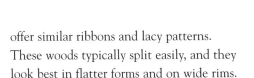

▲ ▶ This log of bird's-eye box elder burl will yield grain similar to this natural-edge bowl.

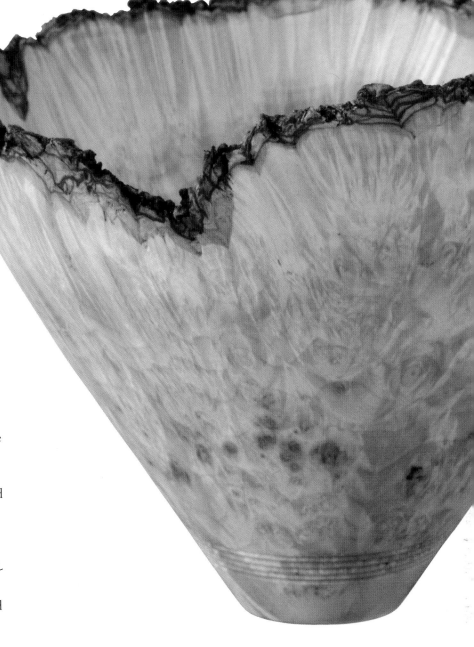

offer similar ribbons and lacy patterns. These woods typically split easily, and they look best in flatter forms and on wide rims.

Ribbons of darker wood wandering across the growth rings, as in the oak pictured at center on the facing page, make for the sort of spectacular patterns in the small bowl made from the other half of the heartwood.

Knobbly logs like the box elder pictured above are always worth pursuing, as the wood should contain burl similar to that shown in the bowl at right. Immediately beneath the bark these logs will often be spiky, like the mallee burl on page 12, which has been sandblasted to remove the bark. This surface was retained for the spiky rim in the bowl pictured at the bottom of the facing page.

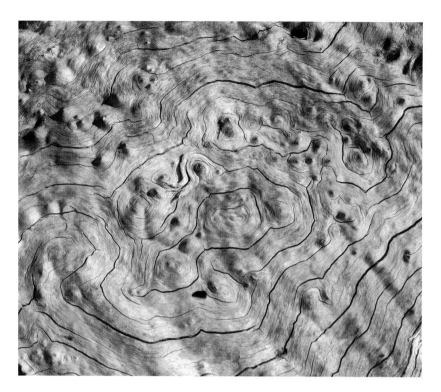

▲ The surface splits following this swirly grain might be 1 in. (25mm) deep, and the wood, being redgum, is likely to be full of internal splits and gum veins as well. But it's ideal for heavier forms.

Beneath swirling surface patterns the wood has to be interesting. Splits might be extensive and deep, yet because they're sinuous, the wood can be ideal for heavier forms.

Where To Find Wood

When I began turning wood in 1970 in England, I could go to any number of small sawmills where I could select seasoned boards up to 4 in. (100mm) thick racked up in airy drying sheds. Because the wood was properly seasoned, I could use it straight away, knowing it was unlikely to warp. And when I needed more, I could purchase more.

Wood is often available for the asking, and it is how most bowl turners acquire much of their raw material.

However, by the mid-1970s, air-dried boards were becoming very scarce, as were those thicker than 3 in. (75mm). Kiln-dried boards were, and still are, available up to 3 in. (75mm) thick, but these are never as pleasant to work as those air-dried, nor are they thick enough for most of my bowls, so my buying strategy had to change. Ever since, I have sought freshly felled logs that I transform as quickly as possible into thick, rough-turned bowls, which I then set aside to season and then finish-turn.

These days you can purchase wood suitable for bowls from sawmills, wood merchants, woodturning supply stores, specialist mail-order companies, and firewood suppliers. A great deal of wood is also just lying around in towns and cities, or indeed anyplace where people are active. It is often available for the asking, and it is how most bowl turners I know acquire much of their raw material.

The nearer the growing tree you can find your wood, the less expensive it's likely to be—at least in terms of cash. Free logs can take a lot of time, effort, and resources before they are converted to blanks you can get on a lathe. But, for me, the hunt is always fun and the effort enjoyable—even when the wood isn't quite up to expectations.

A bowl blank ready for turning is usually a thick disk, occasionally roughly squarish. These don't need to be cut from great slabs of wood. The advantage of being a bowl turner is that you can cut blanks from the short logs, crotches, small burls, and odd chunks of wood rejected by most carpenters and joiners, who demand length. Indeed, in these days of rapidly diminishing forests, when wood has become a dwindling and increasingly expensive resource, bowl turners should make every effort not to chop up long boards prized by furniture makers. And anyway, small chunks are easier to handle than long, heavy boards, especially as you get older.

Sawmills

Since sawmills are, metaphorically, nearest the standing tree, they should give you the best deal among commercial wood outlets. These days, mills tend to process only locally sourced logs. Exotic hardwoods—that is, woods not native to your country or continent—used to be shipped as logs but now are increasingly sawn in the country of origin to add export value and reduce transport costs.

Any sawmill should be able to cut a log to your requirements. However, large operations are seldom keen to accommodate a small order, so the mills most likely to help you are the small ones, where you can oversee the operation and even be of some assistance. Portable bandsaw-mill owner/operators offer on-site custom milling services—a good option if you have a number of logs in your backyard.

The big advantage of overseeing how a log is sawn is that you have control over how the grain patterns lie in your bowls. The downside is the pressure it puts on you, having to personally decide how each cut is to be made. With each pass of the sawblade, new opportunities present themselves and critical decisions must be made on the spot: Should the log be rolled or not? How thick should this board be? The experience can be both intimidating and exhilarating. More on this in Chapter 2.

As good solid wood becomes scarcer, a new breed of urban forester is emerging. Usually one- or two-man operations, these companies get their logs mostly from within city and town limits, recycling logs that formerly would have been buried in landfills and dumps, or burnt. Most of them understand what's valuable to studio woodworkers and maintain a pile of crotches and stumps of interest primarily to bowl turners.

When visiting a sawmill, look at the scrap pile. It's the first thing I do because it's where the bargains are. Even the largest bandsaws can handle only certain lengths, and if the tree-fellers have cut the logs too long, they will be shortened. The often sizeable offcuts that result are usually deposited in a corner of the yard before being dumped or split for firewood. Any trees not from virgin forests should be checked for metal.

Lumber Yards

Usually listed in the Yellow Pages, lumber yards can be found wherever houses and furniture are built. Sometimes these establishments will not have ready means for cutting the

◀ This portable mill, set up in a cemetery, is sawing logs felled on site.

▲ Red gum, slabbed and stacked for seasoning. The sticks between the boards allow air to flow through the pile, while the makeshift roof keeps off most of the sun and rain.

► Waxed bowl blanks, ready to go. All grain-alignment decisions have been made for you when you purchase prepared blanks, but you can get a good idea of how grain and color will lie in the finished bowl.

wood to lengths you can carry away. Their core business is selling sawn boards in large volume to the building and furniture trades, and the wood has usually been kiln dried. You might find hardwoods 3 in. (75mm), even 4 in. (100mm) thick. They generally prefer to load you up using a forklift truck. So if you are driving a station wagon or small pick-up truck, it is wise to carry a saw so you can cut any really long boards to fit. For the less energetic, who avoid handsaws, a small chainsaw, even an electric one with a long extension cord, can be very handy.

Unless the grain is spectacular, short boards less than 4 ft. (1.2m) in length—known as shorts—should cost a lot less per board foot or cubic meter than longer boards. Over the years I've found wonderful bargains in the piles of mill discards. Only rarely have I purchased long boards.

SCAVENGING FOR WOOD

Most neighborhoods have an abundance of useable wood just lying around. Where there is construction, there are offcuts for turning, even in this age of sheet materials. Whenever people have trees in their backyard pruned and felled to let in more light, there will be stock.

Being alert with a predatory eye, you'll be amazed at what you might discover. If you see a tree being felled or relieved of a few big branches, speak to the people doing the job, and they'll likely be happy to let you take the wood; it could save them several trips to the landfill, not to mention fees. I know that even in the blistering heat of Phoenix, Arizona, turners find heaps of useable African sumac, citrus, mesquite, carob, and other wonderful woods that often remain unidentified.

Street trees are cleared for a variety of reasons. The claret ash log pictured on the facing page yielded several dozen bowls,

including four around 20 in. (510mm) in diameter. In an hour three of us sawed it into manageable chunks and loaded it onto trailers. The waste was collected for firewood and the site raked clean.

Many professional bowl turners rely entirely on the urban forest for their wood. All those I know seem to have a good working relationships with local tree surgeons who prefer to drop a log at a workshop door rather than pay fees at a dump.

Many towns and cities have a municipal wood lot where logs go to be chipped or split for firewood. If you can get there first, those logs can be had for a nominal fee.

A photo in the local paper of yourself leaning over a lathe can bring logs to your door. People like their favorite trees to be transformed into objects and heirlooms, so the cost of a log might be a bowl or two, or some treen—a small price to pay for landing something really special that you'd

▲ Check suburban logs for metal. This 12-in. (305mm) cherry converted into a small pile of bowl blanks.

Timbers from old buildings increasingly are being recycled, so recycling yards are worth a visit. You need to watch out for nails, screws, and bolts, and cope with holes and other defects, but these can be used to decorative advantage, and as the world's forests diminish, recycling still-useful timbers makes more and more sense. Recycled wood is often of very high quality, with tight, straight grain, and you know it will be well seasoned.

Specialist Woodturning Stores

Since 1980 woodturning has experienced staggering growth, mainly as a hobby, but many studio turners also earn at least part of their living from the craft. Wood merchants, aware of the proliferation of amateur and professional turners, have made efforts to exploit the

potential market. Many carry a good stock of various exotic hardwoods in logs and billets, and, more expensively, bowl squares and disks. Bowl blanks cut from unseasoned wood will be wax-coated to reduce splitting.

You'll find wood merchants advertising in the many woodworking and hobby magazines, and of course on their own websites. If you're lucky and have an outlet within an easy drive, go and take a good look at their wares before you buy. It could save you coping with splits, but chiefly, sifting through a pile of blanks is exciting, as there is always the chance of discovering something exceptional.

Cut blanks are convenient, especially if you don't have a bandsaw, but all the decisions regarding grain alignment have been made for you. It is also by far the most expensive way to buy wood, and uneconomical for any turner hoping to sell bowls at a reasonable price.

▲ ▶ With a bit of effort turners can haul home a wide range of useful wood for little or no money. In the trailer was my share of this claret ash log—only an hour's work among three of us.

never find commercially. Beware, however, of people offering logs who really want you to save them a heap of work. Don't find yourself making trips to the dump for them at your expense. You're already lowering their costs by removing the heavy stuff.

Since the mid-1980s, hundreds of woodworking and woodturning groups have sprung up across the world. The best known would have to be the American

Association of Woodturners (AAW), which has chapters across the country, but similar groups convene regularly in many other countries. These are worth joining, and not just so you get to hang out with fellow wood fanatics and learn more of the craft; you also get to share the wood that inevitably gravitates to their doors.

Over the years, I have sold many bowl blanks that were gathering dust in the

corners of my workshop and shed. Every one was perfectly usable, but the size or grain or figure never seemed quite right for me or what my retailers wanted at the time. You might approach local professionals just in case they, too, feel like shedding a bit of stock that they seem unlikely ever to use. It's a good way to get going, but soon enough you'll want to cut your own blanks.

— 2 —

PREPARING BLANKS

From Log to Lathe

NCE YOU HAVE YOUR LOG OR boards safely in your workshop, you'll want to make the best use of them. In this chapter I detail how to convert logs into bowl blanks. You'll see how the grain is aligned within a blank and from where in a log each archetypal bowl form or pattern comes. The technique of using various saws in this process is covered in detail in my book *Turning Bowls*.

All wood is a lot easier to work when freshly felled, or green, than when seasoned, so I prefer to convert logs directly into roughed-out bowls as quickly as possible. The other major advantage of working green wood is that you get at it before it starts to split, so you can make better use of your material and even extract good sized bowls from quite small logs.

Once the log is in my workshop, I'll cut about six blanks at a time and rough these on the lathe before preparing any more. These heavy bowl forms have an even wall thickness of at least 10 percent of the bowl's diameter and rarely less than 1 in. (25mm), even on smaller bowls. The roughed bowls are then set aside to dry and are finish-turned weeks or months or even years later, depending on the type of bowl being made. They will warp but rarely split. It is especially important to keep

the grain of a rough-turned bowl fairly symmetrical within the blank, or the bowl may distort unevenly and be difficult to remount for truing and finishing.

If I have to transport the wood back to the workshop, I cut the longest lengths I can heave onto my trailer. This exposes a minimum of end grain, which can be coated with a wax sealer to reduce checking if the wood is not going to be worked within a few days.

▲ To speed seasoning and make better use of small logs, it is common practice to rough-turn bowls. The wall thickness should be even and at least one-tenth the bowl's diameter.

◄ Elm half logs sawn to rough boards and set aside for drying.

▲ Turning blanks cut
round on a bandsaw.

(Various sealants are readily available through
woodturning supply stores.) I cross-cut logs
into multiples of the diameter. You will lose
some width when discarding the bark and
some sapwood, so a 13-in.- (330mm) diameter
log that should yield 10-in.- (255mm) diameter
bowls, is docked into 25-in.- (635mm) and
37-in.- (940mm) lengths. The additional
length is needed to cope with slight end-grain
checking and the width of the saw kerf when
the log is cross-cut again. If you are unable to
convert your log sections straight into roughed
bowls, you should halve them, cleaving or
sawing each along the line of any split. To
help seasoning, then cut a face parallel so you
have blanks like those in the photo on
page 26. With a bandsaw you can take these
a step further, producing disks, ideal for production work.

Logs to Boards

Before you cut a log into bowl blanks, and particularly an older log that has been felled for
some time, you'll need to examine it carefully
for the defects described in Chapter 1. Use a
stiff brush to clean the surface and remove the

dirt from small checks. I use a domestic scrub
brush on relatively clean logs, and a heavy
wire brush to remove thick mud and loose bark.

Dock the end of the log until it's free of all
small cracks. You'll find it easier to examine
the face of the offcut rather than the log itself.
If this reveals defects that cannot be avoided,
repeat the procedure until they are gone. To
seek out the smallest of checks, dock a thin
slice and bend it slightly, as in the photo at
the top of the facing page. Where there is a
defect, the wood will crack rather than bend
in an even curve.

You need to eliminate all minor splits at
each end, so you know exactly what length of
defect-free wood you have to work with. You
will also need to cut out all the splits radiating
from the pith, though most of this is done as
you break down the log into boards.

Bowl-Blank Choices

The orientation of the grain in a bowl can be
manipulated to some extent on the lathe, but
for the most part the patterns you get in your
bowls will depend on how you cut your log
into boards or squares for blanks. Generally,

▲ When docking end grain to eliminate splits, take a very thin final slice and bend it to reveal any otherwise invisible splits.

The grain patterns you get in your bowls will depend on how you cut your log.

the nearer a turned surface lies parallel to the growth rings, the broader the grain pattern.

The main point to remember is that for strength and the best grain patterns and figure, the grain should run across a blank, parallel to the faces, just as it does in a long board. The end grain will be on the sides of the bowl, not in the base.

If you align the grain vertically in a bowl, the end grain in the bottom will be so weak that a hard knock can easily punch a hole in the base. And unless the wood is absolutely dry before you start, retaining the pith will run the added risk of radial splits in the bottom of your bowl. I do not recommend this alignment unless the bowl is less than 2 in. (50mm) in diameter from a blank cut free of the pith.

When working with green logs, it is advisable to keep the grain symmetrical in the blank and the density of wood consistent, so that as a roughed bowl seasons and warps, it does so evenly. (See the drawing on page 14.)

The boards most likely to stay flat are quartersawn, which means they are cut from between the pith and the bark, with the rim parallel to the radius of the log. Bowls roughed from quartersawn blanks will go oval as the

▲ In quartersawn boards, left, the grain is perpendicular to the faces. These blanks will shrink in their width and thickness but not warp. In flatsawn boards, right, the grain is parellel to the faces. These blanks will cup away from the pith.

growth rings shrink closer together, while the rim and base remain flat. Most of the shrinkage is tangential to the growth rings, in the thickness of the blank, so the bowls lose some height. On the end of a quartersawn blank the growth rings run vertically, as seen on the left in the photo above right. The distance between the growth rings has a big effect on the grain patterns within different forms. With widely spaced rings, there will be large areas of bland wood in the long-grain sections, particularly with small bowls; here, the scale is all wrong and tighter rings look much better.

Inside bowls from quartersawn blanks the growth rings run in lines from rim to rim, as seen in the upper bowls in the photo at left. Any color variation between rings will also run from rim to rim. On enclosed forms "eyes" will develop on the long-grain surfaces like that on the right side of the top right-hand bowl. On the outside, growth lines of bowls from quartersawn blanks appear as more or less vertical lines on end grain surfaces. On long-grain areas the lines sag on the concave curves of out-flowing forms, while on the convex curves of enclosed forms, you get concentric rings. (See photos below.)

In flatsawn blanks the grain lies near parallel to the faces. If the center of the base is over the pith, as in the natural-edge bowl pictured on the facing page, the growth rings

▲ The upper bowls are turned from quartersawn blanks, the lower from flatsawn blanks.

▶ ▶ Growth rings in quartersawn bowls are seen as vertical lines on end grain (right), and as loops or rings in long-grain areas (below right).

are seen as concentric rings within the bowl and as a series of near horizontal lines on the outside. Bowls rough-turned from flatsawn blanks will warp, bending away from the pith, as if the growth rings are trying to straighten themselves. The nearer the pith is to the rim of a bowl, the more the rim will peak on the line of the pith. (See the bowls pictured on pages 35 and 50.)

Logs with strong streaks of color or differences between heartwood and sapwood are best flatsawn, so the color is evenly spread across or through the blank. When a streak of sap or strong color runs down one side of a bowl, the visual result is usually less than satisfactory. If the color is across a face of a blank, then you have the option of orienting the bowl to have the color around the rim or as

▲◄ Flatsawn blanks give concentric circles within the bowl that show as horizontal lines on the outside.

▲ ► A Tasmanian sassafras board had the prized black heart across one face. Having the color in the bottom, left, is less interesting than having the color around the rim, right. The outflowing form also makes better use of the grain.

a pool in the bottom of the bowl (photos above). Here, the outflowing form, (right), makes the most of the color and displays the grain better. With the color in the base of the blank (as in the bowl on the left), I needed a nice fat form to display a reasonable pool of grain inside, and even then, encountering it is more a matter of discovery than display.

Bowls making full use of half logs with a marked difference between heartwood and sapwood offer striking patterns that vary with the form (see the photos at the top and center

of the facing page). Turning through the darker heartwood (right) visually interrupts the flow of the dark band. A continuous dark band would look much better. In a similar oak bowl (photo lower left on the facing page) cutting through less contrasting heart and sapwood doesn't jar the eye at all.

On enclosed forms turned from half logs with the pith across the top (as in the photo lower right on the facing page), at least a couple of growth rings will sweep like a roller coaster around the form, echoed on the inside with an eye or ring in the base.

◀ ▲ Differing grain patterns from elm half-log blanks. The central white hole in the heartwood, right, interrupts the flow of the dark band.

▲ Bowls turned from half logs usually work better visually when there is no major color variation between heartwood and sapwood, as in this large oak bowl.

▲ An enclosed form turned from a half log (pith on the top) will have at least a couple of growth rings sweeping like a roller coaster around the form, echoed on the inside with an eye or ring in the base.

1   This 22-in.- (560mm) diameter oak log was felled two weeks before these photos were taken. The end is cut at an angle, and, in addition to the two splits and a few surface checks, a band of pulled end grain (lower left) sustained during felling needs to be cut off. The bark looks solid, but the sap immediately beneath is slightly woolly and soft. Otherwise the wood is hard, with hints of some interesting grain.

2   Docking the end of the log removes all the minor splits and reveals the wood's color.

3   On the fresh-cut end grain only one small heart shake is visible. The growth rings are well defined and slightly wavy, with some interesting color variations.

4   Because the end grain reveals no splits on the outside, I dock two lengths equal to the diameter.

5   I now saw the short logs into thick boards. The first cut is just clear of the radial splits along the centerline, stopping short of the bark. This will save re-wedging the log for every subsequent cut. Next, I saw parallel to the first cut, slabbing the log.

6   I use the slab to support the log for the next cut. After this, I stand the central portion of the log on end to complete the initial cut.

8   This 17¾-in.- (455mm) diameter bowl was turned from one of the flatsawn boards produced here. Note the wavy grain and also the symmetrical shrinkage, as the bowl is centered below the pith.

7   I dock the weathered end from the remaining short bit of log, leaving about 15 in. (380mm) of good log. This log converts to six pieces that are easy to lift and to cut into disks on a small bandsaw.

My ideal bowl log is oval with the pith way off center, like the ash limb-wood seen at left. This enables me to cut thick flatsawn blanks that can be used either way up, as well as flat dishes from the outer flitches. The first cut is near the pith, clear of any splits. Subsequent cuts are parallel to the first.

Where the pith is in the center, as in the photo below, I usually go for two quartersawn boards, top and lower left, which vary in thickness according to the radial splits from center. From a 12-in.- (305mm) long log I thereby get two large blanks at least 10 in. by 3 in. (255mm × 75mm) and two boards that yield two small blanks each. A similar log can be

▲ From a log with the pith well off-center, especially if small, you can cut three thick flatsawn blanks, or one thin and one very thick.

▶ As these offcuts show, a 12-in.- (305mm) long log can be laid out to yield at least two 10-in. by 3-in. (255mm × 75mm), top and left, as well as four small blanks from the two quartersawn boards. Alternatively, right, the log can be cut to eight blanks 5 in. to 6 in. (125mm–150mm) in diameter for natural-edge bowls with the bark retained.

cut, lower right of the same photo, to yield eight blanks 5 in. to 6 in. (125mm to 150mm) in diameter for natural-edge bowls.

The photo at right shows a small elm log cut into squared blanks for 8-in. (200mm) bowls.

On a less symmetrical half log, my options are governed by the large split and growth rings. Offcuts from a 12-in.- (305mm) long elm log, below, show two possible layouts: it could be cut to a 10-in. by 3-in. (255mm × 75mm) blank and two 6-in.- (150mm) diameter blanks, top, or four smaller enclosed forms, bottom.

▲ A small elm cut into squares for 8-in. (200mm) bowls.

◄ These offcuts from a 12-in.- (305mm) long elm log show how the log could be cut to a 10-in. by 3-in. (255mm × 75mm) blank and a pair of 6-in.- (150mm) diameter blanks, top, or four smaller enclosed forms, bottom.

1 The first decision with this oak slab is whether to cut all natural-edge blanks or conventional squares.

2 I decide on a deep, square flatsawn blank, and two natural-edge blanks from either side.

3 The first two cuts are square to the surface between, so to square up the remaining side (and remove the bark), all I need do is lay the blank on one side. Here I could have retained the bark for a natural edge.

4 Out of the triangular sections from each side I cut pairs of natural-edge blanks, first slicing each wedge in half.

5 I then stand each of the resulting four wedges on end so I can cut a flat on the bottom.

6 I use the waste to measure off the width of the blank.

7 And if you don't want the bark, keep the blank on end to cut parallel to the base face. This leaves you with the flat-topped blank, seen at left in the next photo.

8 Make no attempt to cut small undercut blanks like these into disks. It's quicker and safer to turn the blanks round. Mount the left blank on a screw chuck, the right between centers, and proceed from there. On the bandsaw, large undercuts can be supported using a matching wedge to fill any gap between the table and the point where the bandsaw blade enters the wood. (See the drawing on page 41.)

▲ ▶ ▶ To lay out your bowls on the end grain, position a line the length of the height of the log, from pith to bark, so that the bark arches evenly over the line. Then draw a centerline to the pith that bisects this line at right angles, as shown above. Use this centerline to lay out the sides of your blanks, as shown in the photos at right.

Natural-Edge Bowls

The main problem concerning blanks for natural-edge bowls is retaining the bark. The likelihood of the bark staying on depends in part on the species but mostly on when the tree is felled. Bark is most likely to remain firmly attached to a log if the tree is felled in winter, during its dormant period. If the bark comes off, the character of the bowl changes, often for the better.

The blanks should have the grain aligned across the blank, parallel to the outside of the tree. I prefer bowls that have a balanced rim, with the low points on one horizontal plane and the high points on another, as in the bowl pictured on page 31.

Cut a log slightly longer than the diameter of the bowl you want to turn. Then lay out your bowl on the end grain, as shown in the photos above. Cut along the side lines, then cut a flat base at right angles to the centerline, as shown in the photos on the facing page. This tapering blank is for an outflowing bowl. Enclosed forms would have squared sides.

If you're cutting natural-edge blanks on a bandsaw or table saw, ensure that there is no gap between the point where a sawblade enters the wood and the saw table (see the drawing on the facing page). The force of a sawblade on an unsupported portion of a log or board can snap the blank over, and you can easily lose a finger or two.

◄ ◄ ▲ Saw the sides of your blanks, as shown in the photos at left. Finally, saw along the line at right angles to the centerline of your blank, above, to create a flat base.

SAFE SAWING

Any gap beneath wood being sawn must be supported by a wedge to prevent the stock being grabbed by the sawblade.

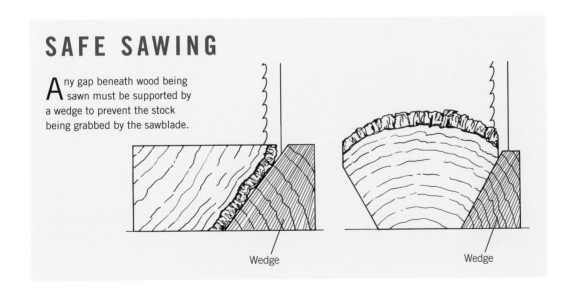

Wedge

Wedge

Burls

Burl is highly figured wood made up of inter-connecting knots and twisted grain. Mostly thought of as lumps that grow on trees, burl can also occur filling in space between buttresses, or spurs, around the base of a tree. Contrary to popular opinion, most burls do have a grain and therefore a grain direction. Because they are built up in layers from a central core, their structure is similar to half an onion sliced vertically through the center. As in other blanks, it's best if the end grain is on the sides rather than in the base.

Hemispherical burls like the caps pictured at left are well suited to single bowls. Simply sliced from a log or tree, they're typically mounted on the lathe without being sawn round. Slabs from large burls are best cut as near as possible parallel to the outside.

▲ Burl caps, such as these in Canberra awaiting export, can be mounted straight on the lathe.

Contrary to popular opinion, most burls do have a grain and therefore a grain direction.

Boards To Bowl Blanks

After the intensive decision-making of log conversion, cutting disks from boards comes as light relief. By the time a log has been reduced to boards most of the decisions about grain alignment have been made, and you are committed. If you purchased the boards, you will have rejected unsuitable material. Now, you'll be anxious not to waste what you've already paid for.

◄ ▲ With some crafty cutting, you can get three bowls from one straight-sided blank, shorter than the sum of the diameters of your bowls.

Normally, I mark out my circles on a board using dividers, and cut out the disks using a bandsaw. This way, I get squat cylinders and the freedom to create any form I want within that cylinder. But if I want to make several out-flowing forms on a small foot, I can get more out of my material by cutting the board as shown in the photos above. Possible bowl forms are outlined on the top edge. This board was cut on a small bandsaw, but I use a chainsaw when working on a larger scale. The angles aren't critical. This is a great way to handle really expensive, unusual, or short boards—I gain one extra bowl for every three cut conventionally. Use the same approach to get two bowls the width of a board where the length is not quite enough for a pair of straight-sided disks.

Don't Forget the Offcuts

When you're cutting out blanks, it's all too easy to toss the offcuts into the firewood pile or trash bin. But there's often a heap of good small blanks hidden in those odd-shaped scraps, and, commercially, I've always reckoned that sales of the small bowls and scoops I make from the offcuts will cover the cost of the whole board, and often much more. With my materials already paid for, the money I get from the sale of the primary pieces becomes icing on the cake.

In the photos at left I cut a couple of 2-in.-(50mm) thick blanks from the remnants of a 5½-in. (140mm) board. The first cuts are across the grain, then the offcut is turned on the large end-grain face for a cut parallel to the original side of the board. As can be seen looking at the bowl outlines on the stacked blanks in the photo below left, the second cut need not create a squared blank. The blanks were turned green, resulting in three 5½-in. by 2-in. (140mm × 50mm) bowls (photo, below right).

Remember that if you cut such undercut squares into disks on a bandsaw, avoid sacrificing your fingers. It is essential that you have

▲▲▶▶ Don't waste your off-cuts. The off-cuts of this 5½-in.- (140mm) thick board (above and right) yielded several 2-in.-high bowls (far right).

▲▲ Often, blanks that hold promise of interesting grain are less than we hope for.

the square upper faces against the saw table or support the blank as in the drawing on page 41. Never have a gap between the point where a sawblade enters the wood and the saw table. It is safer and quicker to mount the square blanks on the lathe and turn them round.

Problem Blanks

Despite our best endeavors, defects appear in blanks, and whether we should have spotted them or not is neither here nor there once the blank is cut and on the lathe.

In some problem blanks we're not sure what the grain or a split might do within the wood. It's worth taking a calculated risk, as with the oak blank in the photo at upper left, which had a few splits that would probably turn away. Nevertheless, it is also possible that a chunk will fly off, which is why you should always wear a face shield and never stand in line with the blank as you turn it. The black line across center is a grown-over knot that could have had some interesting swirling grain beneath, similar to that on this side of the line. However, in the roughed bowl the only hint of feather-like grain is on the rim, where it should be reasonably decorative on the finished bowl.

3

FORM

The Good, the Bad, and the Sublime

A FRESHLY TURNED BOWL OF spectacular color or grain or technical dexterity will draw gasps of admiration, regardless of its shape. But this is no indication of how good a bowl it is. It is the wood or skill of the turner that is being admired, not the bowl. While it is all very well to use grain, color, and technique to stunning effect, these characteristics will never supersede the shape—the most important aspect of a bowl. After the colors have faded and the grain patterns have become obscure, after dazzling technique becomes hackneyed, only the form of a bowl ensures its survival.

By way of confirmation, just about every bric-a-brac store I've browsed has had a few dumpy wooden bowls on which the finish had deteriorated to a point of extreme unattractiveness. All would have functioned well as utilitarian bowls for fruit or salad, and had these bowls a more pleasing shape, someone might have gone to the trouble of having them refinished. But not one of these bowls had a form that might ensure its survival as a desirable object.

Before industrial ceramics changed our lives, almost everyone ate from wooden plates and bowls. Small bowls were used for drinking. Bowls that have survived—some of them for

▲ Inspiring curves are just about everywhere.

◀ Turned green, the profile of this 16-in.- (405mm) diameter oak bowl is grooved to add texture and make the bowl easier to lift, as well as to emphasize the warp and flow of the curves. See also page 63.

centuries—are almost universally beautiful, simple forms. Ill-conceived and ugly bowls must have existed, perhaps in abundance, but few remain. Instead, we inherit those that were treasured enough that, when they split, were patched with metal plates or sewn together with cord or wire. Many are held together with iron staples. These bowls must have been more than simply utilitarian objects.

These days design is all too often regarded in visual terms only, with scant regard to the

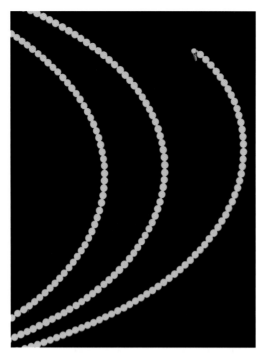

▲▶ Chains hanging between two points (above) always trace smooth curves. Rotated 90 degrees (right) they become ideal bowl profiles for enclosed forms.

▲ The coils of a garden hose create flowing curves regardless of how each is tightened, extended, or reversed into an S-shape (or ogee).

Woodturning always involves curved surfaces. You can't avoid them on a lathe and, unless you confine yourself to turning cylinders and cones, you'll soon find yourself contemplating the subtleties of curves that arc smoothly through a multitude of planes. I will begin by considering curves in their simplest form—as represented by a single line—before suggesting how to apply them to the profile of a bowl, or how they might relate to one another. For the time being, forget the lathe and the roundness it can impart to the simple curve of a profile.

Any line that is not straight is curved. A curve bends smoothly, evenly. It does not have any kinks, flat spots, or abrupt changes in direction. You should be able to feel along a curve without discerning anything other than a smooth transition of altering direction, a pleasure we must all have experienced in our lives when fondling a smooth object such as a pen, a teacup, or a warm body. Or you might have been toying with a glass or some other object and become aware of a slight bump or dip that interrupts the smoothness and jars your senses. If we can eliminate such flaws in our own creations, we are well on the way to making bowls (in this case) that will long survive us.

Let's start with two simple curves. The first, and most obvious, is an arc drawn with a compass. The trajectory of the curve is dictated by the radius of the circle of which it is the circumference. The second is the catenary curve formed by a flexible chain hanging between two points. No matter where the ends are in relation to one another, the curve is smooth and symmetrical. Numerous examples of catenary curves are all about us—power lines, bead necklaces, chains across driveways. These open curves are subject to basic laws of mechanics and gravity and are uncompromising in their symmetry. Such curves can be used on open dishes and bowls, but rotated 90 degrees, these curves become more interesting and suggest possible enclosed forms.

demands of day-to-day use. But because bowls are also handled, the tactile qualities are just as important as how they look and function. It is exceedingly difficult to make a bowl that is a pleasure to handle, that you put down reluctantly once you've picked it up, that you want to pick up again, a bowl that invites your hand to explore the subtlety of balance between the mass of its base and rim—all this in something that must look good while functioning as a practical object.

One of the best ways of seeing what you can achieve with asymmetry is by playing around with a flexible rod or tube. In the photo on the facing page the loosely coiled garden hose illustrates how the line flows easily, regardless of how I tightened or extended the curves.

However, we rarely see curves in isolation or flat; we see them in three-dimensional objects or as part of a landscape. Flowing curves are everywhere in our daily lives, some natural, some man-made, from eroding bars of soap and the fruit we eat, to door handles and the roads we drive upon. The ever-twisting ribbons of cambered highways laid out across our landscapes are sculptures on a grand scale, enormous bas-reliefs. When you see a curve you feel strongly about, try to define why you like or dislike it so much. During the hey-day of the Arts and Crafts Movement many wonderful forms were drawn directly from nature, or based upon shapes spawned by the industrial revolution. In urban areas look closely at buildings, especially the older ones that sport arches or towers.

Inspiration is to be had in wind-blown sand dunes and snowdrifts, or in the curl of an ocean swell breaking on a flat beach. I am fascinated by sensual curves such as these and I try to recreate them in my bowls. And then there are always bodies—of cars and of people. For those who don't care to loiter around the streets gazing at bodies for fear of being arrested, magazines are full of all the raw material you could ever want.

Proportion

Certain proportions have always had universal appeal. Museums provide abundant evidence that, throughout all generations and in all civilizations, similar proportions recur in artifacts and structures. These divisions of space and form rest well on the eye. The use of such proportion can lend an object the kind of presence exemplified in the Taj Mahal or in a fine Japanese tea bowl.

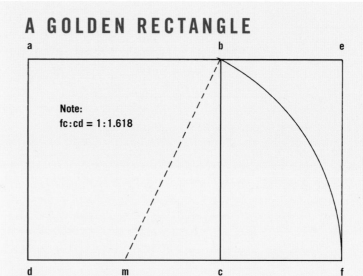

A GOLDEN RECTANGLE

Note:
fc:cd = 1:1.618

The Golden Mean rectangle is easily constructed and subdivided to provide smaller rectangles of similar proportions. To form a Golden Mean rectangle geometrically, construct a square **abcd**. Using **m** as the midpoint of **cd** and the center of the radius **mb**, draw an arc to cut the extended line **cd** at **f**. Then complete the rectangle **aefd**. The ratio of **fc:cd** is 1:1.618, as also is **ef:df**, and **be:ef**. To split any length in similar proportions, simply divide the length by 1.618. Multiply any length by 1.618 to ascertain the larger portion of the ratio. For example: $3 \times 1.618 = 4.85$, or the ratio 3:4.85.

Some people are fortunate to have a built-in sense of proportion that satisfies the rest of us, and are able to apply this without apparent effort to their work. For those of us who are less gifted, there have been a number of attempts over the centuries to define an ideal division of space and form. These generally involve complex mathematical formulae, which I will summarize only briefly, since there are tomes analyzing each system in depth, and a heap of information on the Internet.

Perhaps the most widely known formula is the Golden Mean (or Golden Section) rectangle, which was devised by the ancient Greeks. In this idealized rectangle, the ratio of the short-to-long sides is 1:1.618, which can be devised through several mathematical progressions and geometrical figures. Leonardo Fibonacci, the thirteenth-century Italian mathematician, developed a progression of numbers in which each number is the sum of the two before it: 1.1.2.3.5.8.13.21.34.55.89, and so on. If you divide the number 5 or any

▲ At 6 in. (150mm) high, this oak bowl is almost too deep to be practical at a dining table, although it is used daily as a salad bowl.

number above it, by the number that immediately precedes it in the series, the value approximates that of the Golden Mean.

Problems of proportion recur constantly in bowl turning. Of most basic concern are the ratio of the diameter to the height of a bowl blank, and the diameter of a bowl's base in relation to the bowl's overall diameter. Using a calculator, each can be resolved easily according to the Golden Mean.

However, when I measured the overall dimensions of a number of ceramic and wooden bowls that seem to be universally admired, I found that very few of those over 8 in. (200mm) in diameter get near the Golden Mean. More common proportions were 2:1, 3:1, 4:1, 5:2, and 5:1, which translates to the wooden bowls being turned from standard blanks, typically 6 in. by 3 in. (150mm × 75mm), 12 in. by 4 in. (305mm × 100mm), 10 in. by 4 in (255mm × 100mm) and so on. That the ceramic and metal bowls have similar proportions indicates that other factors to do with practicality and function are involved. In addition, we rarely look at a bowl in profile

(from an angle where we're unable to see the inside), so our perception of the form changes with the angle of viewing, whether we're standing or sitting.

In addition, we are usually too busy getting the most out of our logs or boards, or meeting the needs of our chucks, to take the trouble. Given that it's common practice to cut the largest blanks we can to make best use of a log or board, it is necessary to make the best of the blanks cut, based on the style of bowl being made. For instance, a utilitarian bowl requires a wider base than an unambiguously arty piece that displays a turner's ability to push the bounds of fragility.

I try to bear all this in mind as I turn or design a form, and there are many applications of abstract principles throughout this book—particularly in the following section on profiles. Unfortunately, rigid adherence to such rules of proportion is no guarantee of success. They should be regarded as guidelines that aid your confidence and stimulate your perception of the possibilities, not limit them. Your art is your personal sense of the arrangement of

◄ Decorative beads can be used to define a mass and influence your perception of proportion on a profile.

mass and space. But if you're not quite satisfied with what you've got, you can change your perception of the proportions on a profile using beads or other embellishment to define a mass, as in the photo above.

Form and Function

When the height and diameter of a bowl have been established, decisions need to be made about whether the form needs a foot or not, about how wide the base should be, or if the bowl should even have a defined base. A base does not have to be flat. It can be rounded, or the bowl can be supported by legs.

Manifestly non-functional bowls, like those in the photo at right can have a base as small as you can get away with. Both these bowls need to contain something heavy so they don't blow over in a draft.

The depth and proportions of a utilitarian bowl—even a quasi-utilitarian bowl not intended for use—is dictated in part by its (supposed) function. If you are feeding a large number of people, you need volume, but both

large-diameter bowls and deep bowls are problematic on a dining table. Few dining tables can accommodate dishes in excess of 15 in. (380mm) in diameter. With place settings on either side you'd require a table at least 42 in. (107cm) wide. A standard table is about 36 in. (915mm). So you go for depth. A bowl 5 in. (130mm) deep is becoming impractical on a table because most people when seated cannot see into the bottom. Here's your chance to make a pair of bowls to accommodate greater capacities.

▲ Obviously made to be decorative rather than utilitarian, these bowls need to contain something heavy to prevent them blowing over in a breeze. The natural-edged box elder burl bowl, right, was turned by Dale Nish in 1981.

Profiles

The profile of a bowl is of pre-eminent importance. It is usually the first part to be turned and is the surface to which the rim and inside relate. The quality of the profile always dictates the quality of the bowl. Whether you distort the rim or smother the form with beads and coves, the basic curve and proportion always shows through these embellishments. Good basic form is vital, so how you use a curve (or curves in combination) will make the difference between your bowl looking good, bad, or downright ugly. How you might combine and use curves is a major concern of this book.

Between the (usually) horizontal and parallel planes of the rim and base of a bowl, the side can follow any line you choose—from straight, to a simple parabolic curve, or to some bizarre combination of beads, coves, grooves, and other assorted bits of turning virtuosity. All bowls fall into one of the three main categories: open, enclosed, or cylindrical. (The straight-sided forms present problems of proportion only.) The variations are infinite, although relatively few will really satisfy the eye or offer a form that a caressing hand will leave reluctantly.

The challenge of trying to achieve the right curves in the right proportions continues to fascinate craftspeople in all media. Potters tell me that the beginning and end of a curve are what count; get these correct and you can get away with anything in between. While there's an element of truth in that assertion, I don't agree with the latter part at all. I've started and finished some curves right, and then made a complete mess in between with the greatest of ease, especially where there are beads sitting on the profile.

No matter how near to perfection one solution might seem, it is always possible to find ways in which the form might be improved. It never ceases to amaze me how, over thousands of years, generations of potters, metalworkers, and glassblowers, as well as woodworkers, all over the world have gravitated towards similar bowl forms. I have seen Inca bowls that were made around 1,500 years ago, which are almost identical to ones made in Egypt at about the

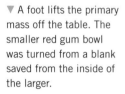

▼ A foot lifts the primary mass off the table. The smaller red gum bowl was turned from a blank saved from the inside of the larger.

same time. Bowls of the New and Old Worlds appear to spring from similar traditions, as do carved bowls from Pacific islands.

After a few thousand years of human endeavor, I can't help but feel that it all has been done before. In these pages you are not likely to find an original form. I might feel that I developed many of them myself, but they are almost certainly variations of well-worn themes. Much of my inspiration comes from ceramics, particularly those of Japan, Korea, and the Middle East, and I am sure this is reflected in many of my bowls.

In the rest of this chapter, I have assembled a variety of shapes to be explored and refined. They are not meant to be the definitive solution to any problem, but rather starting points. Study the profiles and try to understand their underlying principles. Then go to the lathe and see what you can come up with. Trust your eye and check the measurements only if things look drastically wrong. On pages 76–79 are a number of profiles you can use to make templates, which will help you reproduce the forms and understand them better.

The Foot

Before considering the bowl profiles, I must mention the foot—a common element to all kinds of bowls. The word foot is used to define any secondary mass that supports the primary mass of a bowl. A foot is a great device for getting some lift and life into a profile. Feet come in all shapes and sizes (as always) but fall into two general categories. The simplest foot flows into the primary mass of the bowl, as shown at left in the photo on the facing page, bringing visual thrust to the form. Here it is hard to tell where the foot ends and the bowl begins. The second type of foot, on the bowl at right in the same photo, is a separate entity—neither the foot nor the bowl will stand well alone, although they work quite nicely together.

FOOTED FORMS

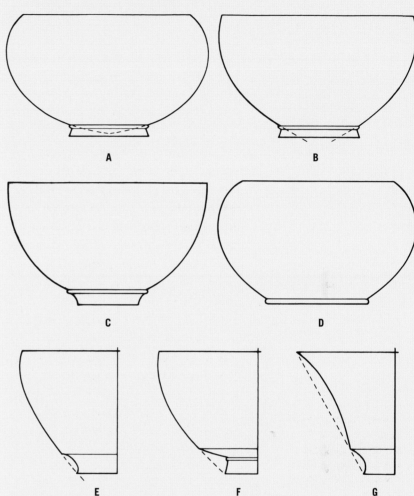

When the full-bellied asymmetric curves of a profile meet within a foot, as in **A**, the bowl seems to sit higher than a similar bowl where the projected sides intersect below the base, as in **B**, which seems to sit more firmly as the lower profile carries the eye down. In **C**, the outflowing foot beneath the hemispherical bowl, makes the form seem higher than the other two. At **D**, too wide a foot can make a form somewhat ponderous. Here, no foot would be an improvement.

Steeper, asymmetric curves are handled differently. The foot looks best where its diameter is determined by the point where the projected line of the profile intersects the horizontal plane on which the bowl sits, as in **E**, **F**, and **G**. At **G**, the corner created by the abrupt change of direction in the wall lies on the line between the rim and foot.

As with all other proportions, these are not hard-and-fast rules, but are guidelines to be absorbed into the subconscious and adhered to only roughly.

PROFILES FROM ARCS

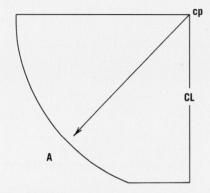

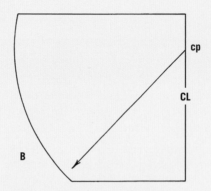

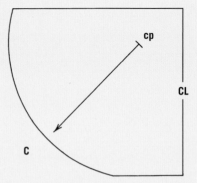

The center point of the arc **cp** is at the center of the rim in **A**. The arc sweeps away from the base well enough but arrives at the rim with a sense of unfulfilled promise. It looks like it was cut off in its prime, before it could run its full course.

In **B**, the center of the arc has been lowered to enable the curve to return slightly at the rim. The rim is much better, but the bottom of the curve is a disaster— the base has broadened to make the form exceedingly stodgy. This is a very common bowl profile, usually resulting from the stricture of an expanding collet chuck or an oversized faceplate.

The solution in **C** is to use a tighter arc with its center below the rim. The diameter of the base is approximately two-fifths of the diameter of the bowl, and the profile bounces in slightly from the fullness of the curve, making the form more restful to the eye. It will also feel better in the hand than either of the others.

SYMMETRY VS. ASYMMETRY—1

Though the symmetric profile based on a tight radius, top, looks good, it is dull compared with the asymmetric curve, bottom.

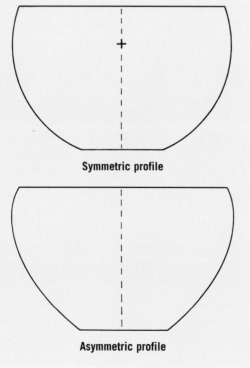

Symmetric profile

Asymmetric profile

Open Forms

Most of the curves in this section flow out-ward, occasionally nearing the vertical, but seldom crossing that line to return toward the center of the bowl. Simple convex or concave curves can be used individually, or combined to create ogees (S-shapes). But remember that the outward sweep of a concave curve, which creates a mood of generosity, can be marred if the profile turns back towards the rim.

An arc is the simplest of curves and will produce the simplest profile. In the drawing above you can see in the half-profiles the effect of three different arcs—all sections of a circle, different because of the location of the centerpoint.

The top profile in the drawing at left is based on a circle and the Golden Mean. The diameter, height, and base are related in the 1:1.618 ratio—(base : height), (height : diameter), (base + height = diameter). As a

◀ ▼ Cherry, 8 in. by 4¼ in. (200mm × 105mm). An asymmetric profile is more interesting than an arc. The bead on the rim adds strength as well as visual effect.

6-in.- (150mm) diameter bowl with a ¼-in. (6mm) wall, the volume of this form would be more than adequate for side salads or breakfast cereals. The fullness of the arc gives a generous form, while the return of the curve hints at containment and reassures us that any wayward contents will be kept inside the bowl by the rim.

Even though this profile looks good, I find it dull next to the asymmetric curve shown below it in the same drawing, which is of the same overall dimensions. The shallow curve at the base springs more dynamically from the flat surface before it tightens near the rim. As a curve resolved, this is altogether more interesting. It still offers a sense of containment and is a favorite form of mine. The cherry bowl in the photos on this page is a fine example. The bead around the rim adds both visual appeal and strength.

Study the profiles and try to understand their underlying principles. Then go to the lathe and see what you can come up with.

OUTFLOWING FORMS

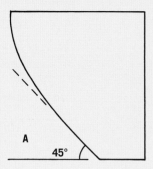

A 45°

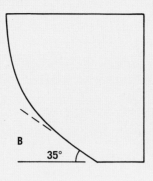

B 35°

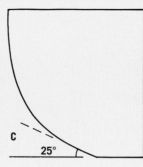

C 25°

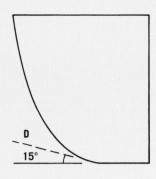

D 15°

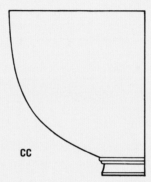

CC

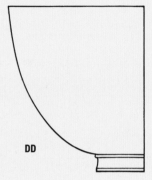

DD

With the tightness of the curve near the rim, in **A**, the form suggests containment, though being slightly top heavy. The steep angle from the base means that if the bowl is knocked over it will remain on its side rather than right itself—not a very practical form.

As the tightness of the curve moves down the side, in **B**, a different feeling is generated. The form is more open as the curve sweeps out to the rim after a tight beginning. Whatever was lost in the sense of containment is offset by the sheer generosity of the form, yet it still conveys a sense of security regarding its function as a container.

As the tight curve descends further, in **C**, the form begins to sag and look dumpy. Such a form can sometimes be rescued, however, by the addition of a foot. At **CC**, the 25-degree angle is steep enough to allow an abrupt reversal into the foot, although the actual tightness of that curve is disguised and softened by the addition of two

beads. The line of the curve flows through the beads, with the slightly smaller lower bead enhancing the upward thrust of the profile.

The curve of **D** lifts off at only 15 degrees, so I have put this up on a cylinder, at **DD**. The upward thrust of the asymmetric curve on the foot makes no attempt to flow into the primary mass, but merely supports it. The bead softens the otherwise stark transition from vertical to horizontal.

In the series of asymmetric curves in the drawing above you can see how the location of the tightest part of the curve affects the form as it is viewed in profile. The position of the curve in relation to the rim and base is largely responsible for our gut reaction to a bowl's form. In such deep forms, the ratio of the height to the diameter demands that the curve rise steeply over a short distance, even on a small base. It is important to place the tightest part of the curve in the upper two-thirds of the profile. As a general rule, the curve should set off from the base at no less

than a 35-degree angle (as in **B**). This should satisfy any subliminal anticipation inspired by an upward thrusting line. If the curve leaves the base at a smaller angle and tightens too quickly (as in **C** and **D**), the form will look slumped and heavy.

In a shallow, open form, where the emphasis is on an outward rather than an upward flow of line, the tightest part of the curve is still best kept near the rim. In the series of profiles in the drawing on the facing page, you can see that the steeper the profile is from the base, the heavier it looks.

SHALLOW OUTFLOWING FORMS

The acute angle at which the curve meets the flat surface in **A** and **B** gives the form its floating quality. In **C**, the tightest part of the curve comes off the base making this form slightly stolid, but nothing like as clumpy and heavy as **D** and **E**. The upward thrust of the curve at **D**, combined with its tightness near the base, makes for a turgid form, but at least it meets the base at a definite angle. The flatter and near vertical curve at **E** makes the form too squat and heavy, and the rounded corner between the base and side is altogether too indecisive and in reality usually looks uncontrolled.

Below each of the profiles at **AA**, **BB**, and **CC** are three standard-variation feet. In each, the upper variation provides a solid base for the primary mass. The middle variation is lighter and leads the eye up and away from the base. In the bottom variation, the foot is too wide and makes the angle between the curves of the foot and the wall too acute.

The bottom foot at **AA** has a thin edge, which is too fragile. It can be thickened, as at **BB**, but this often makes the whole foot too heavy for the upper mass of the bowl. A similar foot works better in **CC** because of the shallower curve that rests upon it—the heavier look of the curve demands more support. The middle solution for **CC** looks less stable, but imparts a good lift to the bowl.

In **DD** and **EE** the addition of a foot does a little to lighten the form. Aesthetically, I'd need a very good reason for a wide shallow bowl this shape; it would have to be for a very specific purpose.

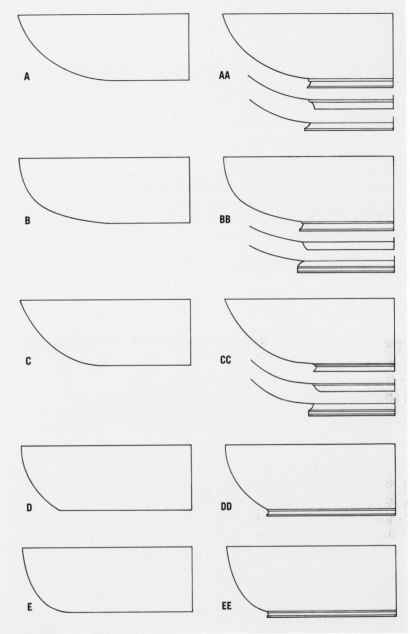

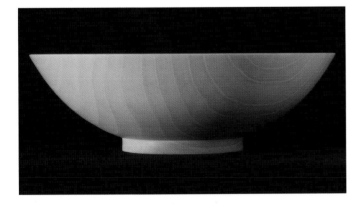

▲▲ The tall cylindrical foot of this 12-in- (305mm) diameter ash bowl remains in sight, viewing the bowl as we would when seated at a table.

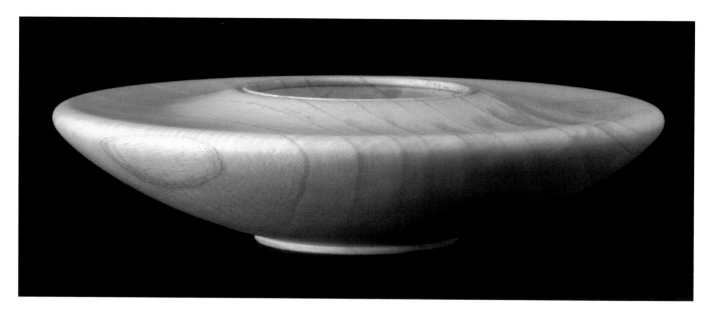

▲▲ The base should be large enough to support the working area of the bowl. On the yew bowl, above, the base is half the diameter. At top, a foot slightly smaller than the hollow of the bowl is all that is needed. Any larger, and the form begins to look chunky; any smaller, top heavy.

Beware of making a foot too small. The foot needs to be wide enough to support the contents of the bowl as in the photo at left. So on the extravagantly chunky form in the photo above, where a fat rim surrounds a small hollow, the foot is only slightly smaller in diameter than the hollow, the containing portion of the bowl. A larger foot will look cumbersome, a smaller will look ridiculous.

Once again, a foot will make quite a difference in the impact of the form, although I don't think that **A** and **B** of the drawing on page 57 gain very much by the additions, at **AA** and **BB**, since they already work pretty well.

Until now, all the profiles have rested on flat bases or a foot, and I haven't mentioned one of my favorite forms—the rounded bottom. The underside of each bowl in the photo at the top of the facing page never quite flattens out. These are the essence of the bowl form. They wobble a bit, but then so do most bowls in the long run—once they've warped a bit, including their formerly flat bases.

Concave Curves

I find concave curves even more difficult to handle well. Proportions are vital if a form is to have a floating quality, without looking either too squat or so light and finely balanced that a puff of wind might blow it away. The two pictured on the facing page succeed.

▲ The bowls above are not quite flat on the bottom, so they wobble a bit. But they never tip over. The large elm bowl, right, was inspired by the traditional dairy and kitchen bowls turned on pole lathes.

▼ The asymmetric concave profiles below combine well with the distorted rims on these green-turned bowls. The grooves on the profile are there to accentuate the distortion and flow of the rim.

In the profiles in the drawing below you can see the real superiority of an asymmetric curve over an arc. Asymmetric curves work well on shallower forms, too, providing good profiles for dishes with flat insides, such as sushi trays and planters. I rarely employ concave curves on thick-walled bowls, as their whole nature implies lightness and fragility. However, the thin rims associated with such forms are particularly fragile on the long-grain sections and liable to break with the slightest knock, so it's prudent not to turn them too thin.

When you are committed to a wide, flat base, as to the right in the drawing at the top of the facing page, these shapes work much better than the stubby, convex curves in the drawing on page 57. Not only do they look better, they function better, too, being easier to lift and hold. There is little benefit from having a distinct foot, since the curves thrust forcefully off a flat surface and create their own integrated foot, as in the bowl pictured also on the facing page.

The line of the profile can be rolled right over at the rim, as shown by the broken lines

◀ The near-flat section of the upper profile combined with the relatively wide base make the larger bowl seem quite dumpy in comparison to the more delicate small oak bowl. The large bowl cries out for a more defined foot, like that of the oak bowl on page 63.

SYMMETRY VS. ASYMMETRY–2

The arcs at **A** and **C** are very mundane when compared to the dynamic, asymmetric curves at **B** and **D**. The latter spring to life as their profiles take off steeply before sweeping outward through the tightness of the curve (creating an integrated foot in the process). Such curves hint at infinity, heading into space on a trajectory, like a comet.

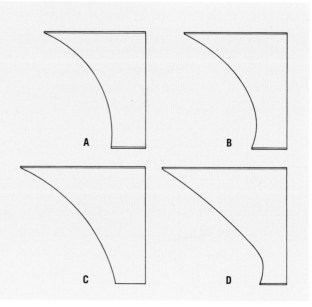

SHALLOW CURVES

Asymmetric concave curves work well on wide, shallow dishes and trays, as at **A**, **B,** and **C**. Less extended, these curves also work well for forms with wide, flat bases, as at **D**, **E** and **F**. None of these forms benefits from a distinct foot, since the curves, thrusting forcefully off a flat surface, create their own integrated foot. A small chamfer makes **E**'s base less vulnerable to damage.

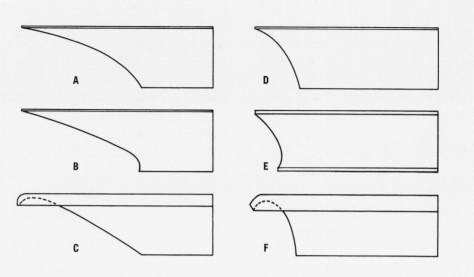

◀ ▲ The rolled-over rim makes this sushi tray easy to lift.

in the drawings above and right. When turning these, beware of creating too sharp an edge on the rim. It's not just the risk of laceration they present while turning; sharp rims are unpleasant to handle, as well as being very fragile. In the drawing at right the line of the profile is barely interrupted at **A**, whereas at **B** the line of the rim needs to relate to the lower curve; otherwise you end up with a fat T. The overhanging rim works best on a larger scale, as at **C**, and especially on a squared-off rim like Vic Wood's dish in the photo at the top of page 62.

ROLLED-OVER RIMS

The more extensive the overhang, the more important is the relationship between the line terminating the overhang and the line of the curve leading to it.

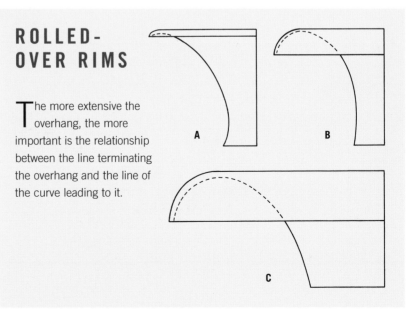

► This 8-in. (200mm) square bowl exploits the potential of an overhanging rim. Vic Wood, 1984.

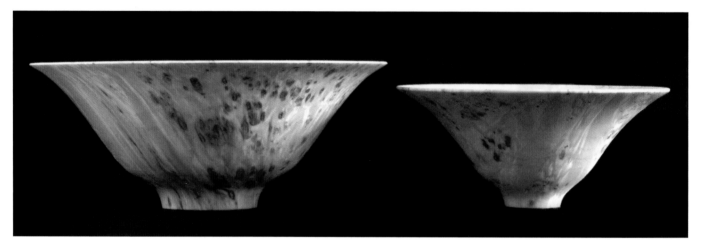

OGEE CURVES—1

The return curve at the base of **B** makes the form at **A** sit more happily.

A

B

▲ An ogee foot emphasizes an outflowing form. Here, the flatter curves of the smaller bowl create softer shadows and the more appealing form of the two. Box elder burl, 6½ in. by 2½ in. (165mm × 65mm) and 4⅞ in. by 2⅛ in. (125mm × 55mm).

Outflowing Ogees

One of the joys and challenges of making bowls in any medium is combining curves satisfactorily into ogees (S- or reverse curves). But when you start flowing one curve into another going in the other direction, things get complicated. If the line moves away at too shallow an angle from the surface on which it sits, the form becomes too heavy. An ogee rarely sits well on its own; it needs to be lifted off the surface.

In the profiles in the drawing above you can see the difference a return curve at the base of **B** can make to form **A**, which does not otherwise sit happily. Better is a curve that rises near vertically off the flat surface, like the foot of each bowl in the photo above the drawing. The narrow foot rises steeply from the surface, and the profile continues to flow upward and outward.

The drawing below again illustrates the importance of the position of the tightest part of the curve (as with the simple curves in the drawing on page 56), but with these S-shaped profiles more can go wrong. An ogee can combine drastically different curves—tight little curls with long almost-flat arcs—or identical reversed curves, and of course everything in between. The options are limitless. At **A** is a good basic form, and at **B** is a good extension of it. You can cut off a curve like this at almost any point and still have a good curve, as you may see in the bowl pictured at right.

The same cannot be said about the other profiles in the drawing. Profile **C** suffers from a weight problem—the convex curve sags, the base is too wide, and the foot is flat and mean. Profiles **D** and **E** are better, though not as good as they could be with the improvements indicated by the broken lines.

One of the joys and challenges of making bowls is combining curves satisfactorily.

▼ An ogee profile tends to look better up on a foot.

OGEE CURVES—2

Drawing **A** is a good basic form. The tight arc of the foot flows into the full portion of the curve and reverses to create a shallow arc, which flows out and up in a wonderful open form. This line can be extended, as at **B**, to create a much larger bowl before the curve drops below the horizontal line of the rim. And you can cut it off at almost any point and still have a good curve.

In profile **C** the convex curve sags, the base is too wide, and the foot is flat and mean. The foot and lower curve of **D** are better, but to eliminate the quirkiness, the reverse curve to the rim needs to be shallower. In **E** the initial descent from the rim is fine, but the convex curve is not quite full enough, which makes the line into the foot too long. The top half of **E**, in combination with the bottom of **D**, would make a good bowl. The broken lines show how each form can be improved.

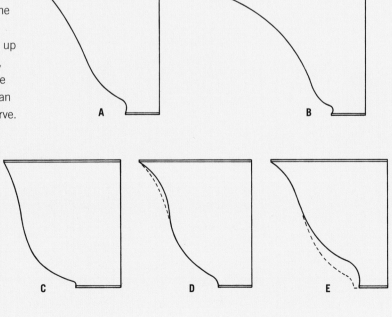

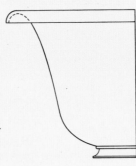
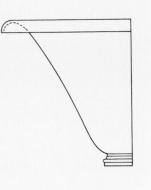

▲ This outflowing foot is tall enough to prevent the bowl looking dumpy. Tasmanian myrtle, 4¼ in. by 3 in. (110mm × 75mm).

If an asymmetric curve reverses and tightens too quickly, especially near the rim, it is easy for the form to become trite. In the drawing above are a couple of examples. The upward thrust is halted and weighed down somewhat by the thick horizontal line—the apparently heavy rim—that the roll-over creates. If the basic curve is good you'll get a nice bowl that displays your technical abilities, but not a particularly exciting form.

In the series of profiles in the drawing on the facing page the ogee is applied to a shallow form. Profiles **A**, **B**, and **C**, where the convex portion of the ogee is low, work well with a foot. Each primary mass sits nicely on its plinth, flowing generously outward. Profiles **D**, **E**, and **F**, where the convex portion of the ogee is toward the rim, are unsatisfactory but not without merit. In each case, the curve that forms the foot doesn't quite work.

The wide, shallow profiles **G** and **H** present two excellent solutions to lifting the primary mass while maintaining stability in a bowl of these proportions. By contrast, **I**, like **D**, with the reverse curve forming a foot, is very stubby and inelegant. As I observed earlier, when you are committed to a wide, flat base, a concave profile like that on the dish on page 61 works better, being easier to lift and hold.

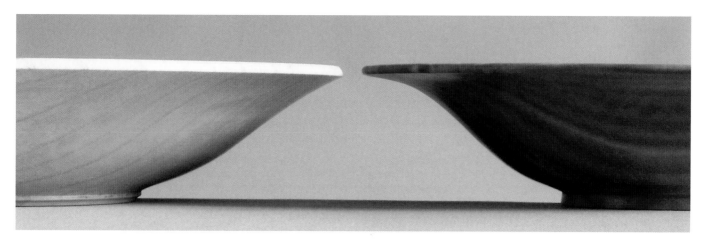

▲ An ogee profile tends to look better popped up on a foot. Avoid ultra-thin rims unless the whole bowl is featherweight.

SHALLOW OGEE PROFILES

Ogees with the convex portion low work well with a foot. Profile **A** would make a practical serving bowl where extra stability is required. Profiles **B** and **C** are much more elegant but less practical, unless the wall is left thick or there is a wide rim to strengthen the form. The long, outflowing line lifts the form beautifully, making each ideal for a thin-walled bowl.

Ogees with the convex portion toward the rim are unsatisfactory. The height of the foot in **E** (indicated by the arrow, where the curve reverses) is too great in relation to the primary mass, making it look unbalanced. The same is partly true for **D**, but its wider base and steeper curve create a profile of uninspiring chunkiness. In a good, safe solution such as **F** the foot is stark and fragile; it should be replaced by a beaded foot like one of those in **A**, **B**, or **C**.

Two excellent solutions for lifting the primary mass while maintaining stability,

the outward thrust of the foot in **G** and **H** prepares the eye to follow the outward flow of the upper curve to the rim. By contrast, the reverse curve that forms a foot, as at **I** and **D**, is very stubby and inelegant. Better would be a more defined foot like those in **A**, **B**, or **C**. But when you are committed to a wide, flat base, a concave profile like those in the drawing at the top of page 61 work better, being easier to lift and hold.

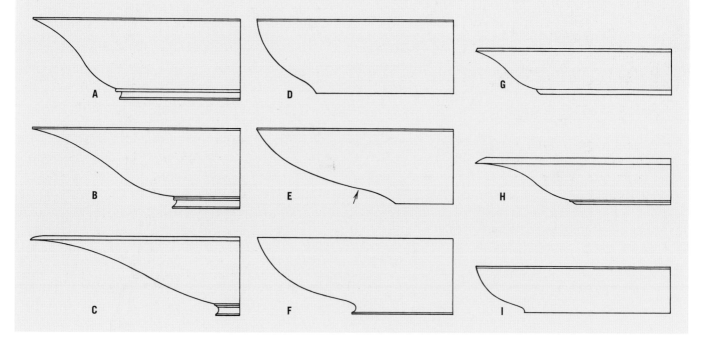

▲ Manchurian pear 6⅞ in. by 3⅜ in. (175mm × 85mm) and box elder 8¼ in. by 4¾ in. (210mm × 120mm), both turned green with rounded bases, both a delight to use.

ENCLOSED FORMS

Profiles in the top row are all strong; the diameter of the base of each is about one-third to two-fifths the diameter of the bowl. Those in the bottom row all suffer from too wide a base and from having the tightest part of the curve in the wrong place.

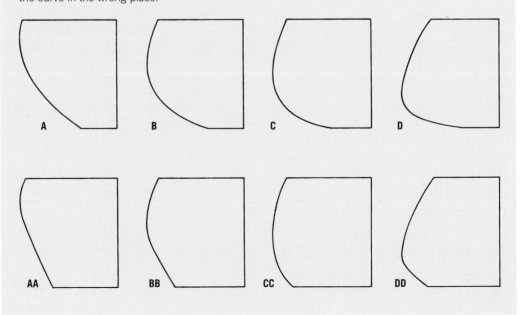

A B C D

AA BB CC DD

ENCLOSED FORMS ON ROUND BASES

These curves, which tighten below the midpoint of the form's height, continue through the centerline, resulting in enclosed forms on round bases—squashed sphere that are sensual to the eye and hand.

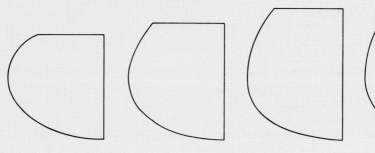

Enclosed Forms

In each profile in this section the diameter of the rim is smaller than that of the bowl. These are containing, even secretive forms.

The top row of the series in the drawing on the facing page shows four strong forms with the fullness of the curve at different heights. The diameter of the base of each is about one-third to two-fifths the diameter of the bowl. These profiles, particularly **B** and **C**, will also work on much wider bowls of the same height, although on a larger scale the results tend to be safe rather than memorable or exciting.

In profile **A**, the long, gentle curve away from the flat surface leads the eye upward before turning back to the rim. This form still visually offers the contents almost as well as the outflowing shapes, whereas **B**, **C**, and **D** enclose the bulk of the contents deep in the form's belly. Salad bowls shaped like these are always popular because the contents are easily tossed while being contained. But all the desirable heavy bits of radish, fruit, and lizard biltong (jerky to North Americans) sink to the bottom and hide beneath the greenery. I prefer the more open shapes for dining, like the bowl to the left in the photo on the facing page.

In the lower row, **AA** through **DD**, are some common variations. All suffer from too wide a base and from having the tightest part of the curve in the wrong place. The steep curve generates no lift to the form and would

be greatly improved by sweeping into a narrower base. My rule of thumb for functional forms of this nature is for the base diameter to be between one-third and one-half the diameter of the bowl, where the rim is equal to or greater than the height of the bowl. (I suspend this rule when the rim diameter is less than the height, and for the less practical vase forms.)

If you take forms similar to **B**, **C**, and **D** and continue the curve through the centerline, you will wind up with round bases, as in the drawing above. These slightly squashed spheres, like those in the photo on the facing page, are some of my favorite forms. The curve flattens as it approaches the rim and also across the base, with the tightness kept below center. The result can be so incredibly sensual that fondling such a form verges on the erotic. The squashed sphere is important for two reasons. A perfect sphere will roll about, even with a lot of wood in the base. And spheres don't look good on a flat surface; their proper environment is space.

A simple enclosed form can be radically altered by the addition of a reverse curve.

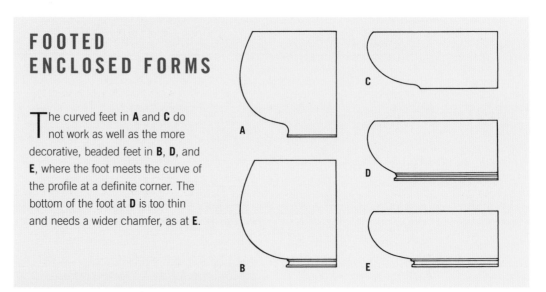

► Gidgee (left) and African blackwood (right), both about 3 in. (75mm) in diameter.

FOOTED ENCLOSED FORMS

The curved feet in **A** and **C** do not work as well as the more decorative, beaded feet in **B**, **D**, and **E**, where the foot meets the curve of the profile at a definite corner. The bottom of the foot at **D** is too thin and needs a wider chamfer, as at **E**.

▼ Oak, 9 in. (230mm) in diameter, with a rounded base.

A foot placed beneath an enclosed form presents many of the same problems encountered with the open bowls.

Enclosed Ogee Forms

A simple enclosed form can be radically altered by the addition of a reverse curve. This creates an ogee into the base or lip of a bowl, or both, yielding a taller form. When the fullness of the curve is in the lower half of the profile, the forms tend to the impractical—not ideal for salads or potato chips—but fine for decorative pieces displaying flashy grain, or as a surface for beads or carving. The proportion of the diameter to the height of the profiles in the drawing on the facing page, about 3:2, is ideal for blanks about 9 in. by 6 in. (230 × 150mm) or 6 in. by 4 in. (150 × 100mm), and works as well in reverse, switching the diameter and height.

▲ Turned in 1991 by Rude Osolnik from near-seasoned wood, the surface and rim have shrunk and buckled somewhat, but the original form remains. Oregon myrtle, 9 in. by 5⅛ in. (230mm × 130mm).

ENCLOSED OGEES–1

Upper curves that reverse enough to flow outward, as at **B** and **C**, lack the tension of the flatter reverse curve that continues inward to the rim, as at **A**. However, an outward-flowing opening implicitly conveys more generosity. The rim of **A** creates an abrupt, less welcoming opening. Like that of a cave or mineshaft, you're not sure what's inside. However, with rounded bases these gourd-like forms are amazingly tactile.

At **C**, the reverse curve into the foot lifts the form, making it more formal and vase-like. An alternative to this reverse curve into the foot is a foot that is vertical or outflowing along the lines of the alternatives at **CC**. The addition of a foot to **A** and **B**, at **AA** and **BB**, indicates how profiles with a low belly seem more comfortable raised by a reverse curve rather than some form of cylindrical foot.

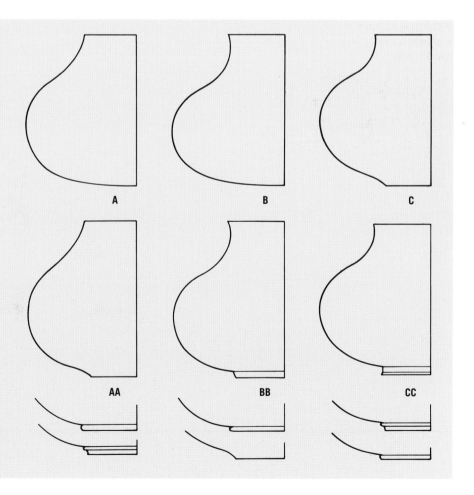

The small reverse curve into the rim makes these 8-in.- (200mm) diameter bowls more interesting and tactile.

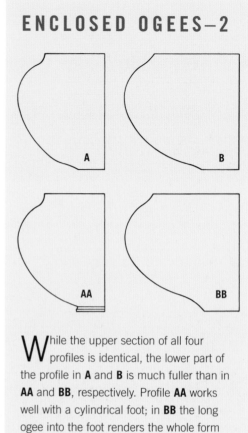

ENCLOSED OGEES—2

While the upper section of all four profiles is identical, the lower part of the profile in **A** and **B** is much fuller than in **AA** and **BB**, respectively. Profile **AA** works well with a cylindrical foot; in **BB** the long ogee into the foot renders the whole form slightly top heavy.

Conversely, in the drawing above, having the fullness of the curve high with just a small ogee into the rim and a lower profile sweeping to a narrow base is more formal.

In the photo top left, we see a similar but better balanced form with the fullness of the curve just above center. Here the tighter curve into the rim, like that to the right in the photo at the top of the facing page, is more appealing than the flatter version at left.

Angles

Let's look at some ways in which the curves on the preceding pages might be combined. The eye will always be drawn to any point on a profile where there is a sudden change in direction. In the bowls pictured at the bottom of the facing page, where two curves meet, a line is created. The meeting of two concave curves, left, creates a more definite line than where concave and convex meet, right. This

◄ Both the Al Gruntwagin, left and Michael Peterson, right, hint at a reverse curve into the base to lift their forms. Note the different openings that define the character of each pot.

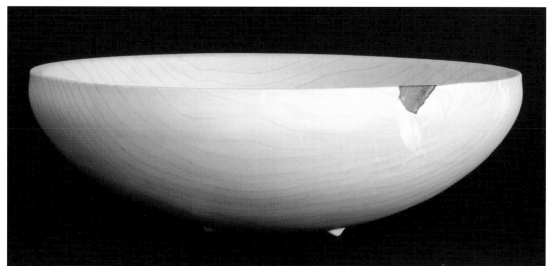

◄ The hint of a reverse curve at the rim brings some generosity as well as tension and energy to this large, 18½-in. by 6¾-in. (470mm × 170mm), claret ash salad bowl that an enclosed form lacks. The bowl sits on three small feet.

◄ The eye is drawn to the line where different curves meet. This line needs to be positioned carefully to avoid the form becoming ponderous.

An example of profile **A** in the drawing below.

line can be hard, or rounded and therefore softer. But either way, it needs to be positioned with care if the form is not to look ponderous. The form at left works fairly well.

In the drawing below are four classic forms. Their quality is dependent on how the points of inflection relate to each other along the line of their profile. In the drawing on the facing page only **A** is a classically stylish decorative bowl, while **DD** is a good working bowl; the rest are proportionally at odds.

COMBINED CURVES—1

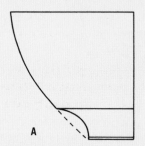

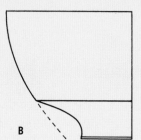

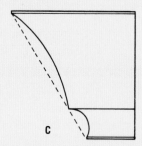

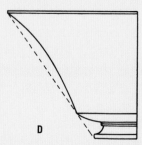

At drawing **A**, the foot is cut into the sweep of the curve. The point at which the profile changes direction and the bottom edge of the foot remain on the line of the curve, which is satisfying. At **B**, the eye is jarred by the foot being arbitrarily positioned; it is too small in relation to the upper curve. Also, the line defined by the junction of the foot and wall is too high, making the form top-heavy and gawky. Where concave shapes are combined, the balance is maintained by keeping the relevant reference points of the profile in a straight line. The top of the lower portion at **C** shouldn't be any higher, and it certainly doesn't look as good as **D**, where the lower portion is one-fifth the height of the whole.

▲ This foot is cut into an otherwise conical profile. The edge of the foot, its largest diameter, remains on the same line as defines the profile.

▲ Plain corners can be too stark for many tastes, so a small bead softens the transition between the wall and rim. Echoing the bead at the top of the foot made the form busy, so I removed it.

◄ The shadow line on this 9-in. (230mm) Tasmanian blackwood salad bowl is softened to make it more tactile.

COMBINED CURVES–2

At drawing **A** the upper concave curve springs nicely away from the tighter convex curve below. At **B**, where the points also lie on a straight line, the delineation between the concave and convex curves is a shade high. On the other hand, the wider base makes for a very functional form that displays the contents. If the curves are reversed, as at **C**, the form becomes top heavy, especially on a smaller base.

The form at **D** always seems to look top heavy. The problem lies in the way the lower portion of the convex curve relates to the foot. The same curve on a wider foot, **DD**, is better, having the look of a good working bowl.

F, **G**, and **H** are also good practical forms, but the oversized cove at **E**'s base makes a compatible or satisfactory internal curve difficult to achieve.

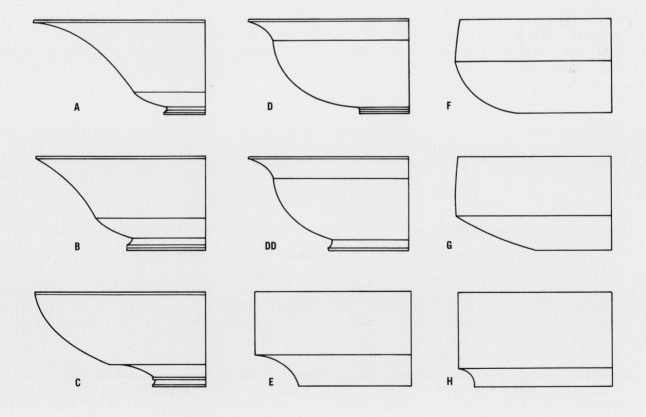

COMBINED CURVES—3

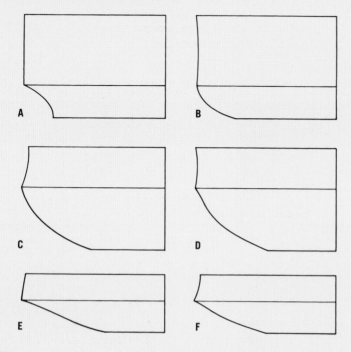

The horizontal at **A** is too high for the concave curve beneath, whereas that same height works well with the convex curve at **B**. The difference between **C** and **D** is very slight. To keep the horizontal line well defined and crisp in **D**, the lower convex curve reverses slightly to an ogee where it meets the upright concave upper curve. (See also the photo at the bottom of this page.) On wider, flatter dishes **E** and **F**, a slight ogee makes lifting a platter easier. These forms usually look better with a foot that also makes them easier to pick up.

The drawing at left shows some chunkier forms. As usual, the inflection point between curves creates a horizontal line in the elevation of the bowl. How we regard the position of that line in relation to the whole depends in part on the curves above and below.

An angle between two convex facets needs careful sanding to preserve a crisp shadow line, although a soft shadow line, as pictured at the top of page 73, is also attractive. Another technique is to slightly reverse the lower convex curve into an ogee where it meets the upper convex curve, as in the photo at the bottom of this page.

The upper surface of an enclosed form is ideal for showing off any interesting grain, especially if the bowl can be displayed at a low level, where it can be viewed from above. On profiles where a strong horizontal line separates two surfaces, some form of detail at the rim of the opening tends to complete the form, as in the bowls on the facing page pictured and drawn.

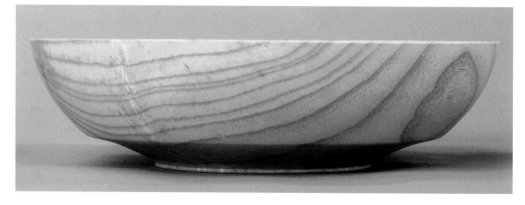

▶ The concave curve into the foot lightens this form both visually and physically, despite the comparatively wide base.

▶ It is easy to round over an angle when sanding. To help define the horizontal shadow line, the upper portion of the lower convex curve in each of these bowls reverses slightly to sharpen the angle between the two surfaces.

◄ A small bead or other detail adds interest to a rim, as well as keeping it from looking chopped off at random.

▲ Like many a classic utilitarian store pot or jar, the neck flares slightly.

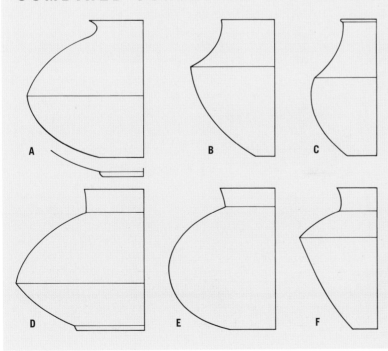

◄ Enclosed forms are some of the best for displaying the wood. Pin oak is not usually this interesting.

COMBINED CURVES ON ENCLOSED FORMS

A
B
C
D
E
F

At drawing **A**, the small reverse curve beneath the rim nicely completes the profile. This implies a thin wall section and a light bowl, despite a hint of heaviness in the base, although not as much as at **D**, which looks almost clumpy. The **A** profile can look better for an outflowing foot, whereas **D** would be better without.

The rim at **B** looks good because the upper curve is flowing out very slightly. Where a similar upper curve is more vertical, as at **C**, a small bead around the rim prevents it looking as though chopped off at random.

In the bottom row, the neck on **D**, **E**, and **F** each provides a vertical rim that terminates the upper portion of the profile. These are definitely containers and (like that in the photo above right) are cousins to the myriad similar ceramic, glass, and metal forms created through millennia to hold our foods and oils. **E** looks good popped up on a foot.

PROFILE TEMPLATES

The profiles in the drawings on these pages are not here just to look at. I suggest you select a few to copy, and that you make templates to help you get the curves right. Don't let the notion of copying bother you; it's an excellent way to learn about form and to develop your eye. In the workshop where I began turning, I was given templates to use for all the standard bowls—for the inside as well as the outside. When I started working on my own, I continued to use templates for all my basic profiles for about a year. As my eye improved, I needed the templates less and less. I was making a lot of sugar bowls and salad sets—consisting of one large and six or eight small bowls—and the practice they provided soon rendered the templates unnecessary.

The templates will be most useful to beginners, although a number of professional turners might want to give them a whirl, too, especially when trying a new form. A good exercise is to make sets of 6-in.- (150mm) diameter bowls. You aren't likely to get complete sets in the beginning, but the effort will almost certainly yield a number of more than passable and saleable individual pieces. It is ironic that by marketing these "failures" to reluctant craft shops in the early years of my career, I created the demand for the limited-production, one-off bowls that I've enjoyed making since the mid-1970s. These days it's difficult to sell

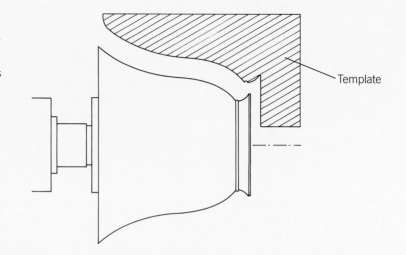

Template

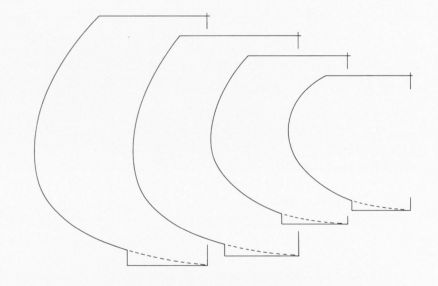

▶ When I turned this 6⅞-in. (175mm) voamboana bowl in 1979, it was bright purple. Within weeks light mellowed the wood to near black. All wood darkens eventually.

batches of identical bowls, such is the demand for "unique" and individual pieces.

These profiles are meant to provide overall line and proportion. Detailing is up to you. If you want to include a bead or two, work out where it or they should go, and cut a slot into the template. The feet have purposely been left square and undefined to allow you to adapt them to your own style. If you are using chucks to close around a foot for hollowing, you'll need to add a foot to those forms without, then turn it off later.

Don't limit yourself to the shapes on these pages; you'll find many others throughout this book and in books and magazines around the world. These are forms on which to build, and from which you can develop.

Make your templates from hardboard or thin plywood, or even metal if you plan to use them for production. The best method is to trace the outline on thin paper, and then adhere this to

To better assess the half-profiles on these four pages, simply hold a mirror on the centerline at right angles to the page. The reflection will reveal the whole form.

▶ The beads could have been cut all the way to the angle, but stopping short and leaving a band creates a finer shadow line.

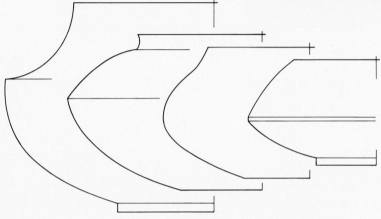

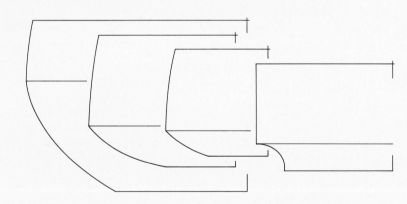

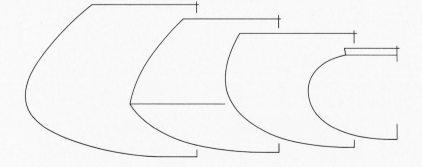

the template material for cutting. (And don't forget that the template should retain the negative shape of the profile.)

Once the blank is mounted on the lathe, true it, and ensure it is free of defects and sawn facets. Next, establish its thickness (which will be the height of the bowl), truing the upper rim and making sure to keep the bottom face flat. If the bottom is concave, you will lose thickness when you cut back to define the base.

Next, establish the diameter of the bowl and mark this on the top face. It is probably better to allow some extra room for your first attempts—perhaps ⅛ in. (3mm) in overall diameter. You can always reduce the curve to the right diameter once it fits the template. Develop regular methods of work. Your forms will be easier to duplicate if you go through the same process each time, and in this way your personal style will develop.

Finally, mark the diameter of the base or foot. With all these measurements set, you can begin turning away the waste to develop your shape. Templates are tedious to use because you need to stop to check so often, but their long-term benefits make it all worthwhile. In the heat of comparing your work to the template, don't forget to *touch* and *feel* the developing form. The quality of a curve is tactile as much as it is visual, and, as your eye develops, so too will your sense of touch.

The quality of a curve is tactile as much
as it is visual, and, as your eye develops,
so too will your sense of touch.

4

WALLS, RIMS, AND BASES

Bowls that Feel as Good as They Look

I

T IS NOT DIFFICULT TO CREATE A wonderful-looking bowl using wood of exceptional grain or color. Or your bowl might have the subtlest of curves creating an exceptional profile using plain wood. Or it might be a vehicle for intricate carving, fluting, or paint. But if your bowl is to feel as good as it looks, as these pieces do, the way the internal curve relates to the profile is going to be crucial. The amount of wood removed during hollowing and the distribution of the wood that remains in the wall determines the physical weight and balance of a bowl.

I hope that the sensations I experience when handling a bowl confirm, at least to some extent, what my eye has programmed my brain to expect. Sad to say, this rarely happens. Sure, a really ugly bowl almost never feels good, but a surprising number of handsome bowls don't feel very good, either. Too many turners strive for uniform thickness (or, more aptly, thinness), which usually results in a boring bowl—all virtuosity but no subtlety or drama. I meet too many turners who seem preoccupied with technique and wood, rather than the design of the objects they make. In a few decades and often sooner, all woods darken almost beyond distinction, unless they are exposed to the weather and sun, in which case

▲ This 9¾-in.- (250mm) diameter bowl is more than an unusual example of pin oak; it is above all a well balanced salad bowl in daily use.

◄ Verdigris Pots, 4¾ in. and 5½ in. (120mm and 140mm) in diameter.

they go silvery. Either way, color wanes and one wood becomes difficult to tell from another. Good form is of paramount importance.

This chapter considers first wall thickness and interrelating curves, then moves on to rims. A rim affects your visual perception of a bowl, its purpose (a rim defines the working portion of the interior); also, the rim affects your sense of touch as you pick up a bowl—does it feel good and fit nicely into your hand, or does a sharp edge dig into your skin. Finally, the chapter discusses bases.

Walls

To my mind, the only reason to make a bowl wall uniformly thin, apart from the challenge, is if it is to be pierced. Then part of the raison d'être of piercing is to display the even wall thickness. Apart from that I see no particular virtue in a bowl wall being either thin or of even thickness, although a combination of both is often held to be the holy grail of bowl turning. All these show is a degree of technical expertise, and that you might own a laser gauge to make the job of turning them easier. A varying wall thickness is usually far more interesting both to see and feel. However, this does not mean that the two curves that sandwich the wall thickness undulate, rather that two flowing curves complement one another.

A practiced eye can see how the inside of a bowl relates to the outside without having to pick it up. Light falling on the inside reveals how smooth or flowing the line is, and its direction. The bottom of the inside is assessed in relation to the surface the bowl sits on, so it is not difficult to spot if a bowl is overly thick in the base from across a room or even in a photograph, as in that below.

The weight and balance of any bowl is dictated by the thickness, or thinness, of the wall and where any variations in that thickness lie. If a bowl wall is much thicker at the rim than the base, it will be top-heavy. Conversely, if too much wood is left in the bottom, the bowl can feel as though ballast has been inserted into its base for extra stability. There is no universal equation for a well-balanced bowl. If a bowl has a wall that tapers to a thin rim, then it is reasonable to expect the weight to be more toward the base. Looking at a bowl similar to that at front in the photo on the facing page, this is what we expect when we handle it, as we might also expect in handling the enclosed form at left. When a rim is not tapered, as to the right in the photo, the phys-

▼ The way a highlight falls on the inside of a bowl reveals the smoothness of the curve and the thickness of the base, also gauged in relation to the surface the bowl sits on. On the walnut bowl (right), which is similar in shape to the upper bowl in the photo at the top of page 84, the highlight on the steep wall stops abruptly where the flat base meets the wall. On the gentle curve inside the lace she-oak bowl (left), the highlight fades gradually towards center.

▲ When a wall tapers to a thin rim, as at center and left, we anticipate the weight to be toward the base. If the rim is wide, as at right, the physical weight is best balanced evenly between the rim and base.

ical weight is best balanced evenly between rim and base.

Achieving the right relationship between the inside and outside curves is at the heart of the bowl turner's art. I can offer no magic formula, but you'll make little real progress without occasionally examining the cross section of a bowl. You can see what is happening when a squared rim exposes a wall cross section, such as in the photo on page 62 and the photos on page 96. Those are easy to analyze. But you learn much more if you cut a few bowls in half so you can examine the complete wall thickness. (These half bowls can have another life, either glued back together to create different forms, or as half bowls with a back to hang on a wall.)

Slicing forms in half is a common practice among apprentice potters, who are fortunate to work with a reusable material. I'm sure it accounts, at least in part, for the large number of excellent thrown ceramic bowls. I suspect

that the contrasting dearth of top-quality wooden bowls reflects the failure of turners to indulge in a similar exercise. I strongly recommend you slice in half any bowl that you know to be inferior; you will learn much from the cross section. What's more, the process will enforce a less precious approach to your craft. Tougher is cutting a good bowl in half, but your courage will be rewarded by an insight into what constitutes a good bowl.

Achieving the right relationship between the inside and the outside curves is at the heart of the bowl turner's art.

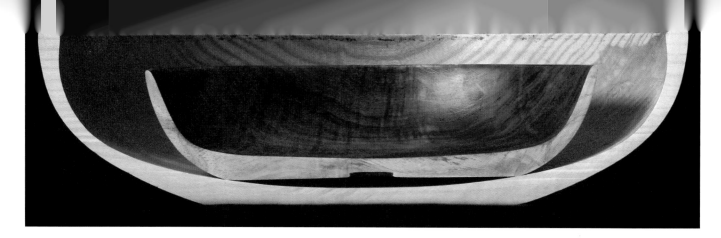

▲ All is revealed in the cross sections of these good (lower, made of ash) and bad (upper, made of walnut) archetypal bowls.

▼ The center bowl has good lines, with none of the bumps and dips that spoil the bowls above and below. There, the drawn lines reveal where more wood could have been removed to fair the curves.

In the photo above are examples of what I consider to be the best and the worst in run-of-the-mill bowls. The upper one—9½-in.-(240mm) diameter English walnut—is one of the first large bowls I ever made back in 1970. (Note the contrast between the freshly sanded wood on the cross section and the darker, oxidized surface elsewhere—wood really does change color.) The lighter, 14-in.- (355mm) diameter ash bowl is one of my standard production bowls from around 1979.

The upper bowl displays several features common in beginners' bowls. Here, the diameter of the base was dictated by the 6-in.-(150mm) diameter faceplate that was used to attach it to the lathe. (The recess in the base

helped locate the faceplate.) The exterior profile is rather innocuous, although it would have looked much better if the curve had swept in more to create a narrower base and had met the base at a definite angle instead of at a sloppy radius. But this bowl really pales when we consider its inner profile—the epitome of everything I hope now to avoid. The shallow V across the bottom meets the wall much too abruptly, leaving too much wood on the rim of the base. Farther up the wall, the curve flattens out again before arriving indecisively at the rim. This is a fine example of a curve that doesn't flow. All together, it's the sort of bowl most novices create.

In contrast, the profile of the ash bowl, below it, rises decisively away from the base, beginning as a shallow convex curve that tightens gradually toward the rim. The internal curve sweeps around smoothly, relating to, but not copying, the outside. No dips or bumps mar either curve. The rim makes a definite statement in an asymmetric convex curve of its own, and the way in which the inner lip is cut back slightly toward the profile creates a shadow within that emphasizes the form.

These bowls contrast even more when handled; the ash bowl is much better balanced. The wall is thinner below the rim, which takes away much of the weight in the upper part of the bowl and leaves a nice balance between the masses of the rim and base. The slight dovetail shape of the cut-back rim also makes the bowl easy to lift using one hand. The rim fits snugly between fingers and thumb, inspiring confidence. The external sweep of the profile makes it easy to lift using two hands since there is

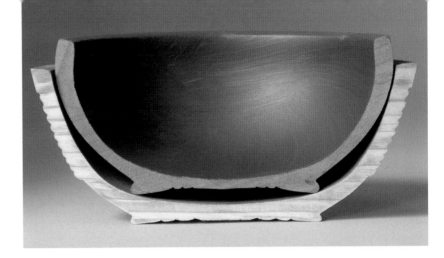

▶ There is little (but significant) difference between the bowl that looks and feels good, above, and that which just misses, below.

enough room to get your fingers beneath the bulk of the bowl. The walnut bowl fails badly in these regards. The sides are too steep to allow the bowl to be lifted easily with two hands. And if you use just one hand, the thin tapering wall and rounded rim will tend to slip from your fingers if you don't hang on tight.

Contrast these cross sections with those in the photo at the bottom of the facing page. At center is a practical bowl with flowing curves that might look better without the small beaded foot. The cross sections above and below reveal less than satisfactory curves typical of so many bowls. On the bottom bowl, the inner curve is fine, apart from a very slight dip at center, which would be difficult to discern running your fingers across the inside of the bowl. On the outside, the line drawn to smooth the curve that flows from the rim to the top of the foot highlights a distinct bump.

The heavier cross section, top, needed more work to develop satisfactory curves, and it also highlights a chucking problem. Inside, the suggested curve was drawn from center to pass through the thinnest point on the way to the inner lip of the rim, making a sweeping curve from a shallow V. Smoothing the curve on the outside reveals a bump toward the base and a straight line toward the rim, although the latter is not so bad. Use of the expanding chuck to grip the bowl for hollowing precludes reducing the diameter of the base slightly for a more interesting lower curve on the outside. If this bowl had been reverse-chucked so the lower curve and base could be reshaped, chances are that the bottom of the bowl would have ended up a bit thin. By contrast, the foot of the center bowl can be removed without affecting the thickness in the base. A chuck contracting around a foot provides a more secure fixing when hollowing, as well as more design options.

The small production bowls in the photo above right were made from similar sized blanks. Each foot fits the same chuck, and

▲ Although moderately chunky, the lower bowl feels better and is better balanced than the one above, where the wall is more even and the whole lighter in weight.

although the curves are without any dips or bumps, the upper bowl looks better—and feels a lot better in the hand. I attribute the comparative clunkiness of the lower bowl mainly to its more even wall thickness, and then to the less tactile upper profile. The beads were intended to be decorative, but they ended up more as a display of technique and added too much weight to the central portion of the profile. The slightly enclosed form of the upper bowl fits better in the hand, and the weight is well balanced between rim and base.

A small-footed form generally benefits having extra weight in the foot for stability. The lower bowl in the photo above has the mass nicely distributed, and, even though a shade thick overall, feels right. The rounded rim

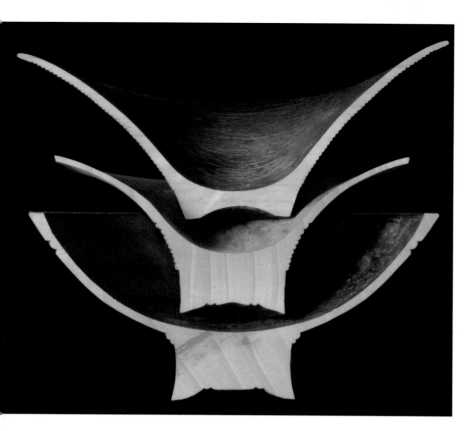

▲ Where the profile is essentially a single curve, walls that taper slightly work best. The walls of forms that sit atop a pedestal foot can thicken toward the rim, being slightly dovetailed in cross section.

brings expectations that the wall will thicken in the base. The simple profile and internal catenary curve is an elegant combination. The natural-edge bowl on top does not feel so good because the top of the internal curve wavers toward a taper but can't get there (because of the natural edge), so what is felt is a slight lump on the higher portions of the rim. The bowl would have felt better had the wall become slightly thinner two-thirds the way down, similar to the upper bowl in the photo at the top of page 85. On the profile, the lower part of the curve straightens a bit to create a definite angle where it meets the curve of the foot, making for a more interesting form than simply tightening the curve into the top of the foot.

Where the profile flows from base to rim in outflowing forms, like the upper two in the photo above, a bowl feels better if the wall tapers to the rim. Here the beads (mainly because of their small scale) do not impact negatively on the bowl either visually or in the hand. The center bowl feels better than the one above for the extra weight in the foot.

Where the bowl sits on top of a foot, as in the bottom bowl, I usually revert to slimming the wall beneath the rim. In part this is because I like wide rims. But a wide rim also adds strength to the form, particularly while it's being turned and sanded. Note the tiny beads that soften the corner between the foot and the profile.

When it comes to enclosed forms, turners often seem preoccupied with getting their walls as thin and even as possible. Turning thin, even walls is definitely a challenge worth accomplishing and probably necessary if you are going to pierce the wall. However, I prefer a bit more weight in these essentially ceramic or glass forms, as in the upper bowls of the photo at the top of the facing page. These pieces are all about 7 in. (180mm) in diameter, so are a nice size to fondle, fitting into a hand as they do. The thin, even wall of the bowl at bottom is impressive for its lightness, but it doesn't feel as good as those above. Top right feels best.

Finally in this section, a word about wide flat bowls similar to those in the photo below on the facing page. Both measure 6¼ in. (160mm) by 1¾ in. (45mm) and are typical of many bowls created by novice turners. Both were fixed on a screw chuck while the outside was finished, and both were prepared for rechucking so they could be hollowed.

On the upper bowl a small bead of a foot was turned to fit the correct diameter for the step-jaw chuck selected. (The jaws won't mar a foot if it is turned to the correct diameter.) The base was recessed slightly so the bowl would sit on the rim of its base, and, once it was hollowed, the bowl could easily have been rechucked to remove the small foot. The cove-like chamfer that links the wall and the top of the bead is there to reduce the mass of wood in the corner between the wall and base with a bit more style than merely rounding over the corner as on the lower bowl. Hollowing the upper bowl was easy because of the wide diameter on which the chuck gripped.

By contrast, the lower bowl was mounted over standard jaws that expanded into the base.

◀ A bit of weight like that in the upper enclosed forms usually feels better in the hand than a lightweight, evenly thin wall. The bottom bowl could be half the thickness again and more of a technical feat, but not necessarily as tactile an object.

Because this offers much less support for the bowl, the work would have screamed with vibration as the bottom became thin, which is why the maker domed the inside, fearful that it was too thin. It didn't help that he cut the rabbet for the chuck deeper than necessary. Nevertheless, the maker could have dished the bottom to remove the rabbet and make the base slightly concave. In fact, he left it slightly domed, so the bowl spun like a flattish spinning top.

Inside, a line shows how the curve could have been a tad fuller in the corner. This bowl could have been reverse-chucked for the base to be re-turned. Lines show how such a base can be dished so the bowl sits on the rim of the base, and the profile improved.

Whenever expanding chucks are used on small bowls, the overall form of the bowl is likely to be compromised. Chucks with good dovetail jaws can grip on a recess as little as $1/16$ in. (1.5mm) deep, but most novices err on the side of caution with a recess depth of $3/8$ in. (9mm) or more. Even if the base is a minimal $1/16$ in. (1.5mm) thick over the chuck recess, the overall thickness of the base is greater than need be. As with the walnut bowl to the right in the photo on page 82, the heavy base will be obvious from a distance.

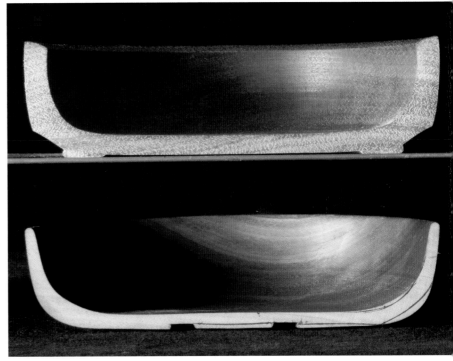

▲ Avoid using small expanding chucks that require a recess (lower bowl), as these make turning more difficult than need be, and frequently compromise the form. Better is to use a chuck that contracts around a foot like that on the upper bowl. You can remove the foot later if you don't like it.

▲ The rim of this 18-in. (460mm) dish slopes in and is slightly concave, with the inner lip slightly undercut. This creates a strong shadow line that defines the working area of the bowl.

▲ Claret ash bowls, each with a curved rim, sloping either inward or outward.

Rim Basics

Dictionaries define a rim as an outer edge, often slightly raised, that runs along the edge of something curved or circular. In bowl terms it is the surface between the hollow of the bowl and the top of the profile, frequently with a well defined inner or outer lip, as in the photo at left. The slightly undercut inner lip creates a shadow that further defines the inside, working space of the bowl.

Turned rims can be divided into four general groups: level, inclining inwards, inclining outwards, and rounded. Each of these can be made thick or thin as well as convex, concave, or ogee-shaped. Non-turned rims can be natural-edged (with or without bark), carved, or square. Once shaped, a rim can be textured, painted, or otherwise altered. So experimenting with rims can occupy a lifetime and yield infinite variety.

Whatever its form, the rim of a bowl is linked inextricably with both the inside and the outside walls. A rim defines and often frames the working space of a bowl. A good rim can attract the eye while encircling secretive depths or fabulous grain; or it can create illusions of thickness or thinness, or look so inviting that the urge to touch it is irresistible.

Rims deserve far more attention than they get. Too often the top of the bowl wall is cursorily rounded over, or otherwise vaguely or carelessly executed. The lower bowl in the lower photo on page 87 is a fine example, where the maker was happy not to have gone through the bottom, and, anxious to complete what would be his third bowl, didn't attend much to the rim beyond getting it smooth. Given the tapered wall, this might have been the best solution. The rim on the upper bowl has more style, whereas my early walnut bowl, on top in the top photo on page 84, is a fine example of a rim I hope you'll avoid.

As our confidence at the lathe grows, we tend to turn better-defined rims with an inner and outer lip. At this stage of a turning career

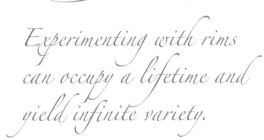

Experimenting with rims can occupy a lifetime and yield infinite variety.

▲ Three classic rims, each one suiting its respective form.

it is not uncommon for edges to become dangerously sharp, even on finished pieces. These are never comfortable to feel when you're handling a bowl, so should be softened as sanding proceeds. Edges can be crisp without being razor sharp.

If I have one ground rule when designing a bowl, it is to avoid straight lines. As a result, all my rims involve curves like those in the lower photo on the facing page, where the two on the left slope out, and those to the right slope in. The broad, deep rim, bottom right, makes the form more decorative than the others, which are manifestly utilitarian.

In the photo above right are three simple rims on top of classic forms. At left the wall tapers, so the rim is simply rounded over. Where there is a small curve at the top of the profile, as on the pot, rear, a convex outward-tilting rim with a well defined outer lip works well. Inside, this creates a soft shadow that shows up the rounded internal form, while the outward-tilting rim catches the light as it casts a bit of shadow underneath. The salad bowl rim, right, is very slightly convex; this feels better than a flat or concave rim when you hook your thumb over the rim to lift the bowl. Note how the slightly enclosed form creates shadow internally. This makes the bowl look more practical as a container than the more open form to the left, although in use they function equally well.

Enclosed forms usually benefit from having a collar, like those in the two lower photos at right, to link the profile and the opening. Whether or not a couple of small beads support the cove, the opening is defined. A simple detail looks good on most enclosed forms.

▲ Box elder, 9 in. (230mm) diameter. The cove strengthens the rim, as well as adding interest and emphasizing the slight warp, as intended.

▲ Enclosed forms often look better for some detailing at the rim.

RIMS TO GET YOU STARTED

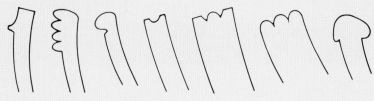

Rims on near-vertical walls

Rims on
enclosed bowls

▲ Beads can be used to
strengthen a rim or decorate
a surface near the rim. The
bowls above are about 9 in.
(230mm) in diameter.

Rims provide an opportunity for you to display your turning skills, and here are a few to get you started. The less sanding, the better, as excessive use of coarse abrasives leads to uneven wall thickness.

I avoid flat rims: at the very least the top of any bowl wall I turn will be slightly curved, usually convex, and angled either in or out. If you put beads on or just below a rim and decide you don't like them, you can turn them away. Or even use power-sanding if the wall is very thin. Beads on a curve look best when the curve flows smoothly beneath, as though the beads were added later.

Any fine detail on top of a rim, like the four to the right in the top row, needs to be turned before the wall begins to flex: set the thickness of the rim by starting to hollow, but cut in no more than ½ in. (13mm), and turn the beads or coves before completing the internal wall. Never try to cut fine detail into a flexing wall unless you want to have the bowl explode and risk hurting yourself.

On very thin-walled bowls, a narrow rim can almost vanish visually, offering no obvious edge to the bowl. The cove in the rim of Jim Partridge's green-turned holly bowl, photo top right, effectively casts a defining shadow within itself in all but overhead light. Another trick is to color the rim, as in the photo center right. These rims were blackened using a permanent marker, so each stands out in almost any light.

Wide Rims

Wide rims provide more of a frame for the contents of a bowl than do narrow rims. A wide, plain, flat rim—where the inner and outer lips are in the same horizontal plane—tends to be uninteresting unless eased by coves, beads, or some other form of decoration. Terry Scott turned a wide flat bead into the flat rim of his large dish, photo below, which he then covered with tapa cloth. There's more about tapa on page 145. The inward-tilting rim on the smaller bowl,

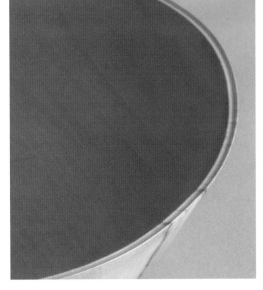

◄ The tiny cove on the rim of Jim Partridge's 7-in.- (180mm) diameter holly bowl provides a crisp frame to encircle the interior.

▼ A simple way to make a narrow rim stand out is to color it. Simplest is to use a permanent marker.

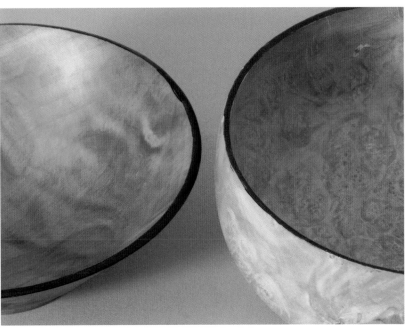

▼ The black on the rim of Terry Scott's large pohutukawa dish is inlaid tapa cloth that has been stained and wax-polished.

▲ On chunky bowls an inward sloping rim can be widened by reducing the working space. The inner lip needs to be well-defined.

▲ A bead creates some interest on this flat rim.

▲ ▲ A wide rim makes large bowls easier to pick up. The inner lip of a convex rim is best undercut to create a better defined angle and stronger shadow line. From the side, each rim could have been an addition to an open bowl.

photo above, is effectively relieved with a bead that breaks the flat surface. In this situation, ensure that the surface on which the bead sits flows beneath the bead, as though they are separate elements.

As you can see in the photos at left, a rim can tilt in or out as well as be thick or thin. When you need two hands to lift a large dish or bowl, a wide rim you can get your hands under helps.

But while a wide rim makes a bowl easier to pick up, a couple of practical points need to be considered. First, avoid very sharp corners. Sharp edges are uncomfortable to hold and, with careless handling, can even cut skin. Always soften sharp edges with a dab of fine abrasive; 240 grit does the job. And second, don't leave the rim too thin if there is the slightest chance of the bowl being picked up by the rim, especially if filled with something relatively heavy, like fruit. I've seen thin rims

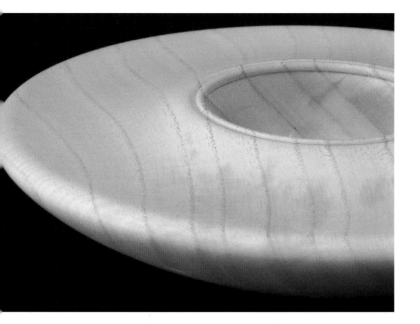

▲ The nice little bead on the inner lip defines the small working space of this near-solid form. The groove on the inner lip located the expanding jaws of a chuck. (For a full view of this bowl see the photo at the top of page 58.)

Beads on a curve look best when the curve flows smoothly, as though the beads were added later.

▼ Beware of making a rim too fragile. These rims are strong enough to lift the bowl by, even filled with fruit. On the lower bowl, beads at the base of the rim bring visual interest. On the upper bowl, the drawn line suggests an improved profile with a small groove to define the bottom of the rim.

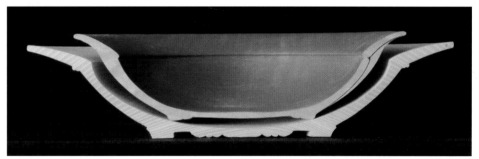

OUTFLOWING RIMS

held across the grain break when jerked into the air, so I leave a reasonably substantial rim that can take the weight, as in the sawn bowls above right. On the lower bowl, a couple of beads in the corner between the profile and the rim bring visual interest where the bowl wall ends and the rim begins. The heavier section of the upper bowl would look better if the underside of the rim were lengthened, as shown by the drawn line to the right. Here the bottom of the rim would be defined with a small groove, echoing the demarcation on the inside.

On the more sculptural and near-solid form in the photo above left, the rim looks best with low-angle lighting that reveals the concave surface. The bead on the inner lip defines the inner space, and provided a fixing point against which I expanded a chuck so I could round off the back. A thin-walled variation of this form is at front right in the photo at the bottom of page 88.

On wide and flatter rims, beads and angles can be used to define the working space of a bowl. On a profile use beads to add strength in the corner between the profile and the wide overhang while softening the angle. Complete the top of the rim before you start on the inner wall.

▲ If natural edges are balanced with the high points in one horizontal plane and the lower points in another (as at left), a bowl looks good from any angle. When the high and low points are not balanced (as at right), the form may look good from only one vantage.

▲▲ The overall saddle shape of the rim creates an illusion that the bowl is oval rather than round. On a shallow form like this, the dip in the rim furthers the illusion.

Natural Edges

The urge to retain the bark of a log or the spiky surface of a burl is almost irresistible, especially if it's free of defects. On forms like those in the photo at left I aim to have the rim balanced so the upper points are in one horizontal plane and the lower points in another. If the valleys or low points are different depths, a bowl tends to look fine from one side only. If the upper points are not in the same plane, the form invariable seems unbalanced.

A blank cut from an evenly round log yields a bowl with a saddle-shaped rim, like the ash bowl at left. Though this bowl looks oval, it is actually round. Like the bowl at right, many burls have a spiky surface beneath the bark which, if removed, reveals a rim that evokes a mountain range; this is a far more interesting rim than the bark-encrusted one on a similar box elder bowl in the photo on page 21.

For the best chance of retaining the bark, a tree should be felled in winter when the sap isn't rising. Some logs will dry satisfactorily retaining the bark, but the inner bark (adjacent to the cambium layer of the sapwood) shrinks dramatically more than the wood. This means that when turning a natural-edge bowl from wood that is not fully seasoned, if you want to ensure a smooth surface between wood and bark, you need to rough-turn the bowl and leave it at least a couple of weeks. Then remount the bowl and complete the job—as I did making the elm bowl, two views of which are pictured at left. As usual, the overall saddle shape makes this bowl seem oval-carved rather than turned. The dramatic dip in the rim enhances this illusion when you look down on the form. From the side you see sweeping curves highlighted by the darkness of the bark. You also have a nice contrast between the coarse rim and the smooth interior.

Cutting blanks for a bowl like the box elder at right in the photo top left can be wasteful of material. Better use can be made of burls

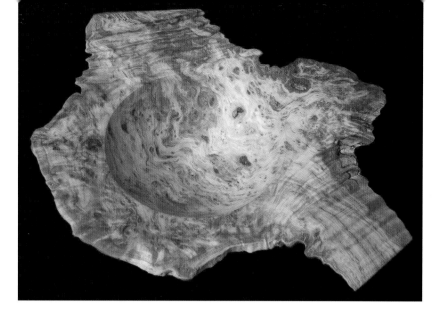

small enough to go straight on the lathe with the cut surface against a screw chuck or faceplate. This fixing enables you to get the most from a burl with a bowl that is often small in relation to its wide, flat, and often very eccentric rim, as on the Tasmanian myrtle bowl in the photo top right. Like any thin overhanging rim, these can tilt up, or down as on the red mallee bowl in the photo lower right. Here the small cove on the inner lip is a nice detail. The pale sapwood highlighting the edge is a real bonus.

A close cousin of the natural edge is found in the rough-sawn surface of a board or block. A sharp chainsaw leaves deep, cleanly cut grooves that can make for an interesting texture, as in the bowl in the photo below. Double cuts that leave a board less than flat can be used to good effect on a jagged rim, leaving a lump like that on the far rim.

▲▲ Flat rims with a natural edge are often spectacular. The Tasmanian myrtle burl, top, is one half of a burl that grew around a branch. On the rim of Terry Scott's mallee root-burl, above, the contrasting sapwood is a bonus. The small cove detailing the inner lip defines the inner space of the bowl better than the simple angle on the myrtle.

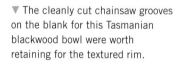

▼ The cleanly cut chainsaw grooves on the blank for this Tasmanian blackwood bowl were worth retaining for the textured rim.

▲ I prefer asymmetric rims on square-rimmed bowls, and usually sand at least two edges so that vertical and horizontal surfaces roll one to the other (as at the front corner), while retaining the original turned thickness (as at the left and right corners).

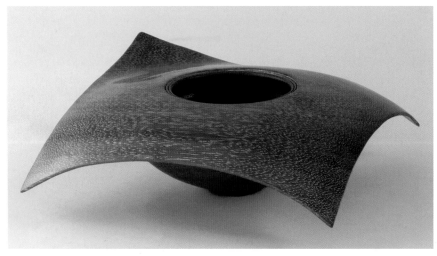

▲▲ Terry Scott's "Ray Bowls" are turned with pairs of wings on each corner, four of which are then cut and sanded away to create the sting ray allusion.

Square Rims

Square-rimmed bowls present many of the same challenges as turning natural edges, and they seem to lure turners like flames do moths. I find truly square-rimmed bowls—those that viewed from above are symmetrical—little more than vehicles for technical display, unless something is done to them. They need mounting accurately on the lathe, and that's about it. Turning flat natural edges or square rims is always hazardous, as it's inevitable that you'll stick a finger in the way of an on-coming corner. That's always painful. But you can turn square blanks safely by gluing up waste blocks to each side, then cutting a disk that encloses the square. You turn the disk, then cut away the waste and finish the four edges. This technique cannot be used on natural-edge blanks.

I prefer to create asymmetric edges as in the photo top left, in part so I can work faster, less precisely, and more interestingly than symmetry entails. This blank had very rough-sawn edges that had further distorted in drying. I decided to keep the side with the nick (to the right). I usually shape the sides, sanding them to something other than a cross-sectional view of the turned rim. Consider the front left edge, which is as it was turned on the left end, with square lips top and bottom. From there the upper lip softens then vanishes, so the inside of the bowl rolls into the lower edge. The same happens on the opposite side.

Terry Scott's "Ray Bowls," in the two lower photos at left, are turned with split corners (that look like a V when spinning), four of which are then cut and sanded away to create the sting ray allusion. A rim can be extended to support the bowl, as in the photo at the top of the facing page. The longitudinal format of this very formal piece makes it ideal on a side-table or even an altar. Gordon Pembridge goes a few steps further, in the middle photo on the facing page, piercing the asymmetric legs he kept from the rim. With any cut and pierced

▲ ▶ Rims can be extended to lift the bowl off the table. Terry Scott's solid-rimmed "Golden Bowl," above, is formal and stylish, whereas all that remains of Gordon Pembridge's rim, right, are the rather menacing pierced legs with their arachnidan overtones.

FAT BOWLS

Very heavy rounded forms with no defined rim and often rounded underneath are more of a challenge than they might appear. That challenge is mostly aesthetic. There being no diversion like an extremely thin wall or other obvious technical virtuosity, curves have to be just right for the forms to succeed visually. These are also tactile objects that demand stroking and might look even better cast in metal. Small versions that fit nicely into your hand with the feel of a water-tumbled stone, like Michael Peterson's off-center turning at right, can radiate stillness in their apparent simplicity.

▲ Michael Peterson's 8-in.- (200mm) diameter bowl, like a water-smoothed stone, is wonderfully serene.

▲ The edges of this rectangular red gum bowl, 12 in. by 8⅝ in. (305mm × 220mm), are textured to contrast with the smoother surfaces above and below.

▲▲ The undulating rim is a cleaved surface, as split from the log. The rim is blackened to define the cleft top and natural edges on two sides. The remaining sides are the remnants of the square blank sanded.

rim, a uniform wall thickness is essential for overall composure, as are flowing curves. Cutting into a rim highlights every bump and dip that even rounding and distorting the edge cannot hide.

Squarish bowls can also be somewhat monumental in weight, with rims and sides that offer surfaces to embellish. The edges of the redgum bowl, photo above, were textured while it was still on the lathe (but definitely not spinning), using a small electric chainsaw. The spindle must be locked to hold the bowl firmly in position for such work. A Dremel tool could have been substituted for the chainsaw, producing different marks. The idea is to have rough sides that contrast with the smooth surfaces above and below. The grooves inside are mainly to define the working space of the bowl, but the top groove also located the expanding jaws of my chuck when I reverse-chucked the bowl to turn off the foot.

The undulating blackened rim of the maple bowl, two sides of which are pictured at left, is a cleaved surface as it was split from the log, then burned with a gas torch, wire brushed, and oiled. To obtain the sharp definition between the unburnt side and black top, the side was sanded after the burning and brushing. This, like other undulating edges, presents a totally different aspect on each side.

INSIDES

've always found it curious that bowls that are less than smooth inside, let alone with turned decoration, are particularly difficult to sell. It's my theory that because most of our distant fore-bears ate from wooden bowls for generations, they developed a gene that leads us to expect that the inside of a bowl should be smooth for reasons of hygiene.

Sadly, few turned bowls are used these days, but that should mean that a flat and grooved inside bottom like that in the small-footed decorative bowl in the photo at right, is more acceptable. It is certainly a more interesting interior than a

▲ A decorated flat bottom is framed by the deep inner wall. Tasmanian blackwood, 9-in. (230mm) diameter.

◄ The grooves were made with a thread-chasing tool, the sets spaced by eye rather than precisely, to give the piece more energy. These grooves decorate a working space defined by the inner lip of the rim.

▼ Here the sets of grooves define the working space rather than frame or decorate it. Claret ash, 15⅜ in. by 3¾ in. (390mm × 95mm).

simple round. On a large bowl designed for fruit, photo above, the grooves help air circulate around the contents and keep the fruit in good condition. This set of grooves was made using a thread-chasing tool (though they're not threads).

On the large and heavy form in the photo at right the inside curve is a gentle ogee from a chamfer that serves primarily to remove the otherwise sharp corner between the inside and profile. The grooves in this bowl define the working space within a wide and smooth band that becomes the rim, even though there is no well-defined angle between that and the interior.

Bases

It is amazing how many people will look first at the underside of a wooden bowl and then, with barely a glance at the form, pronounce judgement on the skill (or lack thereof) of the maker. To be fair, most of these souls are woodturners, checking that the bowls are "properly made"—whatever that might mean. These days it is rare to see screw holes in the base of a bowl, as most turners now use one of the self-centering four-jaw chucks that were developed in the late 1980s. Evidence of how a bowl was fixed on the lathe does not appall me, as it seems to so many other turners. However, I do prefer not to see felt disguising a rough surface. I look for a well-finished base, sanded to the same standard as the rest of the bowl. Screw holes can be plugged simply and cleanly or even disguised as inlay.

Decorating the base of a bowl is not necessary, but it shows that the maker has paid as much attention to that surface as to the others. Most turners today, like many of former centuries, develop a signature decoration like a particular style of bead or a pair of lines within which to write their name.

In the photo at the top of the facing page are the bases of three run-of-the-mill bowls. Each was completed before the bowl was hollowed, and each foot was turned to fit a specific chuck—like most of the footed bowls in this book. When the hollowing is completed, that's it. When I was in full production, not having to re-chuck bowls to finish the base saved me hours each week.

On very small bases I typically have an inset dome, as at left, and on larger diameters some inset beads. I rarely use expanding chucks, as they severely restrict your design options. But when I do, mostly in demonstrations, I keep the recess or rabbet for the chuck as shallow and narrow as possible, like that to the right. The rabbet for chuck jaws need be no wider than the minimum width required for the jaws you are using and rarely much more than 1/8 in. (3mm) deep. This is the underside of the sushi dish in the photo on page 61. On such a wide base it pays to retain some mass within the foot, partly for physical balance, but mostly to make hollowing the bowl less traumatic. A few beads across the central dome pretty it up a bit. The idea is to disguise the fact that the recess is really a fixing detail.

The clutch of bases in the photo lower right on the facing page are on bowls that were reverse-chucked to remove a foot. The base in front is rounded, whereas on that to the right, Vic Wood turned a cone into the foot of his square bowl (see the photo on page 62) to confuse the technically oriented. This bowl was turned within a disk of scrap wood, so the job was easy to reverse-chuck to complete the base before releasing the bowl by cutting away the waste-wood.

When making bowls from green wood, I know they will warp, and that's why I make the bases round. However, not everyone can cope with a bowl that might wobble slightly on the table, so for these folk I carve away most of a cylindrical foot to leave three small bumps on which the bowl can rest, as in the photo lower left on the facing page. Then, no matter how the form warps, it will always sit firmly.

Decorating the base of a bowl is not necessary, but it shows that the maker has paid as much attention to that surface as to the others.

◀ ▼ The base deserves the same attention as the rest of the bowl. Where bowls are taken straight from the chuck, left, I aim to disguise that fact with detail. Below, the front bowl has a slightly rounded base, being turned green. To the right, Vic Wood turned a cone into the base of his square-edge bowl (see the photo on page 62) to tease those preoccupied with technique.

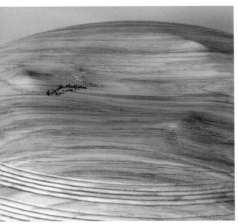

▲ On green-turned bowls that I want to sit flat, I carve away most of a cylindrical foot to leave three barely discernible feet.

— 5 —

GREEN-TURNED BOWLS

∿ *Working with Warp*

PERHAPS THE BEST THING OF ALL about turning green wood is that you can create a top-quality bowl in less time than it takes to make just about any other object in wood. The bad news is that working green wood thin demands that you're either pretty handy with a bowl gouge or prepared to work very laboriously.

Rough-turning bowls to speed up seasoning is standard practice for modern bowl turners, who then remount the dry, distorted bowls on the lathe and re-turn them. This is so customers get a round bowl that sits squarely on a table without wobbling. I began rough-turning green wood in the early 1970s, but it was several years before I realized that there was no reason why I should not completely finish a bowl, even though the wood was unseasoned. Soon after that I discovered that by aligning the grain carefully in the blank, you can be fairly confident of how the bowl will look after it has dried and distorted.

As a bowl turner, then working in England and making conventional bowls, I used mostly ash, cherry, and sycamore for their stability. When rough-turning bowls that would be re-turned, I needed stable wood, because the less I needed to turn away to true up a bowl, the larger the resulting bowl would be and the higher the price I got for it. A severely warped

▲ The vertical edge catches the light, highlighting the undulating rim on this 9-in.- (230mm) diameter Tasmanian myrtle bowl by Andrew Gittoes.

roughed bowl will be dramatically smaller when trued, so has to be priced down accordingly. I soon learned which woods to avoid for making symmetrical bowls, but of course these later proved to be ideal when dramatic distortion was the goal.

If you turn a bowl from unseasoned wood, chances are that it will warp and it might also split. However, generations of turners over at least 1,500 years (according to Robin Wood in his wonderful book *The Wooden Bowl*) circumvented these irritating traits by choosing and cutting their wood carefully. To create the

◀ "Small Entropy," 2006; 6 in. by 4 in. (150mm × 100mm). Bill Luce reckoned (correctly) that a patch of grain on the originally round bottom would collapse enough to tilt the form and create a base. This is one of a series studying how pieces get energy from sitting at an angle, and where the distortion is most effective. The direction and location of the wrinkling is critical, as is maintaining enough of the turned form to define this still as a bowl rather than a gourd or seed pod.

Ash, sand-etched, 11¾ in. by 4½ in. (300mm × 115mm). Turned from a tree felled three weeks earlier, this bowl has barely warped in the year since it was made.

utilitarian bowls that stay near round, these generations of woodturners used woods known for their stability and not prone to warp excessively. In Europe these included alder, birch, and the maples (the acer species), and to those I would add cherry and ash, which I have turned by the tonne with few problems over many years in three continents. Bowls turned from these woods, like that in the photo above, barely distort if you keep away from the pith of the tree and choose straight-grained, knot-free blanks. Select the right wood, and you can turn and finish a bowl using unseasoned wood in the expectation that it will distort very little.

Increasingly since around 1980, "turned green" has come to refer to the practice of turning and finishing bowls in unseasoned wood with the intention that they should distort to anything but round, and often the wilder the better, like the Tasmanian myrtle "Wavy Bowl" in the center of the photo on the facing page. The burl for these bowls had been harvested about six weeks earlier in early spring. It was still very wet when I turned it.

"Rusty Verdigris," 9½-in. (240mm) diameter. The very bland knot-free green wood stabilized after microwaving to provided an ideal palette for faux finishes. The gouache gold line provides a boundary between the two surfaces.

The center bowl distorted so extravagantly because it is burl turned very thin and the rim is outflowing. The other bowls, being more enclosed, dried less dramatically.

In the early 1980s green turning was in vogue for a few years, and all manner of would-be turned "art" flooded the craft galleries. Worse, an eager public devoured it. Too many of these early green turners were content, it seems, to let their bowls warp any old way in the hope that they would prove quirky enough to sell. The fad passed as turners became preoccupied with smoother, slicker, surfaces, so that now, twenty-five years later, I am still disappointed by how few turners have realized the potential of turning green wood. I suspect the reason partly is that turning thin bowls from unseasoned wood requires a good set of turning techniques, because you cannot afford to vacillate, procrastinate, or otherwise dawdle. A thin bowl warps as soon as it's turned, so there is no time to make slight adjustments. You need to know what you intend to do and go for it without hesitating.

Anybody who has worked with wood knows that most woods shrink, split, and twist as they season, so the first question is usually "but won't the wood split if you turn a bowl from green wood?" The answer is, probably not, provided you cut your blank judiciously from the right kind of tree, that was felled out of the growing season. The second question is usually, "but won't the bowl warp if you make it from green wood?" To which the answer is, probably, but so what if it does?—the design opportunities are worthwhile. How a bowl warps is predictable, as this depends on how the grain is aligned within the blank and the shape you turn. For dramatic distortion you need a wood known for its volatility, a wood that when thin likes to warp but not split, like Tasmanian myrtle, most eucalypts, most burls, most oaks, or the madrone burl used by Bill Luce for his "Small Entropy" on page 102. To make the most of what will happen when the wood dries out, you need even-grained material aligned precisely within the blank and on the lathe. Even then, the hardest part is to come.

▲ The Tasmanian myrtle burl for these bowls was harvested six weeks earlier. The center bowl's excessive distortion is due to the thinness and shape of the outflowing rim. The bowls were dried in a microwave oven.

Not all distortion is aesthetically pleasing.

▲ Turned from green jarrah burl in the mid-1980s, the surface of this heavy 11¾-in.- (300mm) diameter bowl has buckled like dried leather. It was originally oiled, and has been wax-polished very occasionally.

▼ Pin oak, 17¾ in. by 4¾ in. (455mm × 120mm). To obtain an even distortion, the pith is across the middle of the top and the wood is of even density. The beads emphasize the distortion, also making such a large bowl easier to pick up. The three feet ensure the bowl will always sit squarely on a table, even when changes in humidity cause it to change shape.

After the bowl has distorted, you must cast a critical eye over the result and destroy inferior pieces, as discussed toward the end of this chapter. Not all distortion is aesthetically pleasing. A reputation for quality is built upon rigorous culling—rather like animal husbandry.

Seasoning

Green-turned bowls should never be finished on the lathe but rather after they have dried. Sealing the surface impedes moisture leaving the wood.

The time required to season a green-turned bowl is, as with all wood, dependent in part on how thick it is. However, we are dealing with bowls, where the center of a block of wood has been removed, and this inevitably alters the stresses within that block. It is not unusual for bowls made from extremely well seasoned boards (air-dried for fifty years) to warp when hollowed. Hollowing is likely to lead to distortion in many woods.

Very thin bowls will usually stabilize in a couple of weeks, even if the base is a relatively thick ½ in. (13mm). I expect larger bowls, like that in the photo at the top of page 104, to stabilize in about six weeks. The large salad bowl in the photo below, with its ⅝-in.-

(16mm) thick wall, took five months to dry, while the much heavier 2-in.- (50mm) thick dishes in the photo above it or the one at right needed nearer eighteen.

That was all air-drying. However, if a bowl fits into my microwave oven, I cook it to speed the drying process, achieving in a few minutes what otherwise takes days or weeks. You get to know almost immediately if your bowl is a splitter, or indeed not going to change shape much at all. It's near instant gratification—or disappointment, whichever the case may be. Unfortunately I've found that microwaving is effective only where the wall thickness is less than ½ in. (13mm). Thicker bowls have to air-dry over months.

Know Your Wood

Your first task when turning wood—and green wood, in particular—is to get to know and, hopefully, understand your material. You must be able to predict what it will do as it dries. Not all woods are suitable for a given style of bowl, and as stated above there are horses for courses.

If you want a utilitarian bowl that has only a slight warp, choose a wood known for its stability, wood like teak, iroko, or mahogany. Chances are they will be fairly bland, but warping won't likely be a problem. What warping does occur will have to do with taking the tension out of the wood as you remove the center. If you want dramatic movement, look for a wood notorious for twisting as it dries, like an oak or casuarina (Australian pine to some Americans), holly, and madrone. These woods tend to shrink unevenly, because of the high differential between their rates of tangential and radial shrinkage (a ratio available in wood technology books and on the Internet).

To ascertain how a wood is likely to distort as it dries, turn a thin test bowl about 4 in. (100mm) in diameter. Leave the bowl in the sun for a few hours, or cook it in a microwave oven for a minute. If it hardly moves, try

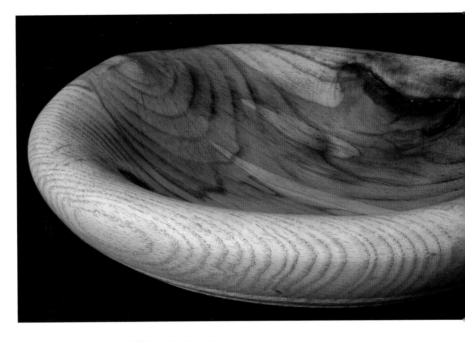

▲ This heavy oak bowl, 13¾ in. (350mm) in diameter, took eighteen months to air-dry and stabilize. Had it been thinner, there might have been greater distortion around the knot.

MICROWAVE DRYING

There are no hard-and-fast rules for microwave drying because the time depends on the precise moisture content and thickness of the wood. Never leave a bowl cooking unattended, in case you pressed the wrong buttons, or it's not as wet as you think. When a wet bowl gets hot, it sizzles; you can hear it. If it dries out and starts to char, you can smell it. If you hear sharp cracks or smell even a hint of burning, cut the power immediately. I've never seen smoke in a microwave, let alone flame, but I've had a number of bowls with burn marks, so they must have been close to igniting.

When a bowl comes out of the microwave, I want it to be almost too hot to handle. Keep the bowls clear of all ferrous metal until they are dry, or risk staining the wood from the contact. Put hot bowls on wood or glass to cool, not a saw table. I usually lay bowls on their side for maximum exposure to the air as they steam off.

As a rough guide, I find that small, very thin bowls, say 4 in. (100mm) in diameter, need only about 50 seconds on their own, and maybe 2 to 3 minutes in pairs. I always set a microwave oven to cook on full power. The four small Tasmanian myrtle bowls in front in the photo on page 105 were cooked together for three minutes—after which they were too hot to hold. The largest bowls I can fit in my microwave oven are 16-in. (405mm) diameter. The bowls at the bottom of page 110 and the top of page 111 had two or three sessions of four or five minutes, cooling between each session.

◄▲ Ebonized Tasmanian myrtle, all approximately 6 in. (150mm) in diameter. The grooves inside the bowl are to emphasize any distortion; the ebonizing is to transform the material so it is less obviously wood. It is the same myrtle burl as in other myrtle bowls in this chapter.

TURNING GREEN WOOD

When conducting workshops or demonstrations, I have found a widely held belief that turning green wood is somehow different and much more difficult than working seasoned material. In fact, freshly felled wood is turned using the same tools and techniques as seasoned wood, but green is much easier to cut and more fun to turn. The downside is that you and everything else in line with the blank gets soaked as the moisture sprays from the spinning wood. So there is nothing especially mysterious to the turning; even grain alignment, as discussed above, is no big deal. In essence, turning green presents only two real problems: finishing and, if the wood is thin, coping with its fragility before it dries.

Wet wood can be difficult to sand because the abrasives quickly become clogged and soggy. Some woods are worse than others, but friction soon dries the surface enough that you can work through the range of abrasives much as usual on dry wood. Cloth-backed abrasive is superior to paper-backed, as the latter tends to

You don't have much time to mess around with very thin walls.

disintegrate with the damp. I have several sheets of each grit in use, so some dry as I use the other. Once the clogged dust has dried a bit, it is easy to remove by rolling the abrasive over the edge of the lathe bed, then twisting it back and forth.

Be aware that the metal in some abrasives will discolor many light-colored woods or those high in tannin. Certain pale woods, such as holly, are more susceptible to this than others.

Wet/dry abrasives are another solution, but remember that electricity and water don't mix, and most lathe manufacturers might not recommend the use of water near their machines.

The need to support a bowl wall becomes more acute as it gets thinner.

A thin wall turned in wet wood is very fragile and flexible, and is easily destroyed by the slightest pressure from the tool or when sanding. There are two ways to cope with this, but before you try either one, finish-sand the outside. This gives you an exact surface to which the inside can relate, and will leave you with less sanding at the very end, when the bowl is most fragile and starting to distort.

The best approach is to use one hand for support behind the bowl wall to absorb any pressure from the tool or abrasive. I generally cut the entire wall down to around ¼ in. (6mm), and then take two cuts as quickly and fluently as possible to arrive at the final wall thickness. You don't have much time to mess around with very

This green-turned "Frangipani Bowl" by Gordon Pembridge warped slightly, adding more character to the undulating bark rim. Such bowls look terrible unless the wall is of even thickness. The bark will usually stay attached if the tree is felled in winter.

thin walls—the wood starts to move the moment it gets thin. Keeping the wood wet by spraying water on it doesn't help. You get only one shot at any wall less than ⅛ in. (3mm) thick, and you need to get on with it. The best way to develop the required speed is to rough out a lot of green bowls, using a small gouge and trying to get the best possible cut with each pass.

If you lack the speed or nerve for making the final hollowing cuts in one go, you will have to go step by step, turning the bowl wall to the required thinness an inch (25mm) at a time, retaining enough bulk on the inside to prevent the form warping. You still have to complete the turning within an hour, as even bowls that are not hollowed change shape when the wood is unseasoned. If it warps before you complete the sanding, lower the lathe speed so your hands can follow the surface, or turn the lathe off and power-sand with abrasive disks mounted in a drill. An angle drill is easiest to handle. For detailed information on turning bowls, see my books *Turning Bowls, Turning Wood,* or *Taunton's Complete Illustrated Guide to Turning.*

another species. If it twists dramatically, it could be just what you're looking for. If the blank was quartersawn, the bowl will go oval. It's worth testing how easily it might bend, break, or split. If it's strong, use it.

The way a bowl warps is dictated by the grain alignment within it, its shape, and how the two relate. How far it warps depends on the species and how green—that is, unseasoned—it is when it is turned. Trees felled in summer contain more water than they do in winter, so their wood will take longer to season.

Symmetrical Distortion

To get any bowl to warp symmetrically, you need the grain evenly balanced in the blank, the center of the tree aligned with the center of the blank and thus with the center of the bowl, as in the photo at the bottom of page 106. The oak log for this bowl, seen in the sidebar on pages 34–35, was nearly ideal; it was straight-grained, of even density, with the pith in the middle. I cut a length from the log equal to its diameter and then cut it along the pith. That cut face became the top of the bowl and the surface to which I attached a faceplate. (Cutting a disk from a half-round slab on a bandsaw is dangerous, so I took another

▶ On green-turned bowls I prefer a near-flat but still round base like that to the left. It's not absolutely stable, but near enough. Before finally truing a flat base like that to the right, be sure that the wood has stabilized.

▼▼ Despite the dramatic distortion of the thin wall, the foot of this 16-in.- (405mm) diameter "Oak Wavy Bowl" became somewhat oval but stayed near flat, requiring only one push on a 240-grit sanding board to level the base.

cut parallel to the first to create a flat face on which to rest the blank as I cut it round.)

The tightness of the growth rings in the center of the rim reveals that little was lost from the top face. The nearer the rim is to the pith, the more dramatic the distortion is likely to be. This is because the distance between the growth rings, and therefore the volume of material between the growth rings, increases the further you are from the pith. Most shrinkage occurs tangential to the growth rings. (Radial shrinkage is typically half that of tangential shrinkage). This means that, as the wood dries, the tangential shrinkage pulls the form down either side of the pith to create the

boat-like form. Think also in terms of the growth rings trying to straighten themselves as the wood dries.

With this sort of bowl there are three options for the base. The oak bowl has three carved feet similar to the one pictured on page 101. One foot is beneath the pith, the other two spaced evenly to either side. Alternatives are a rounded base, like that to the left in the photo at the top of the facing page, and a flat base, seen to the right. When the bowl has stabilized, a flat base needs to be re-flattened. Chances are that you'll be able to do this with a few pushes over a sanding board. (A sanding board is a flat board, like MDF, with abrasive glued to it.) For a very uneven base you'll need a hand sander or hand plane.

On a more outflowing form, such as that pictured in the two lower photos on the facing page, the sides will pull down a little more to create a classic saddle-shaped bowl. This and the oak bowl in the photo top right, required only a single push each over a sanding board to flatten their bases. Although the rims distorted wildly, the bases went oval.

When a bowl rim is turned flat, plain wood will warp to long smooth curves, as in the oak bowl, pictured top right, whereas burl is more likely to become frilly, like the smaller Tasmanian myrtle bowl in the photo below it.

Forms that are enclosed or have near vertical profiles at the rim should become oval, like the lower bowls in the photo bottom right, whose openings went from round to 4½ in. by 5½ in. (115mm × 140mm) and 3⅛ in. by 3¾ in. (80mm × 95mm) after about three minutes in the microwave oven. Bowls in which grain density varies will distort erratically, like the ebonized bowl above.

▶ If the wood is of even density, enclosed forms go more obviously oval, like the oak bowls, below. The ebonized burl, above, varied in density, so the hoped-for oval was distorted, but still acceptable.

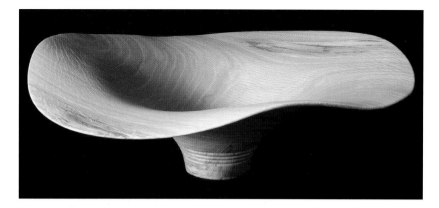

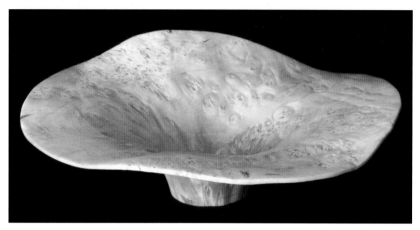

▲▲ Distortion is dictated partly by the wood and partly by the form. On near-flat rims, plain grain like the oak, top, warps to smooth-flowing undulations, whereas burl, like that used by Andrew Gittoes for his 9-in.- (230mm) diameter Tasmanian myrtle bowl, above, goes frilly.

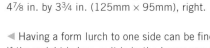

▲ Pin oak "Pot," 6 in. by 4¾ in. (150mm × 120mm), left. Tasmanian myrtle "Calabash," 4⅞ in. by 3¾ in. (125mm × 95mm), right.

◄ Having a form lurch to one side can be fine if the weight is low, as it is in the larger vessel. The smaller is top heavy and off-balance both visually and practically, and is easily toppled.

After the bowl has distorted, you must cast a critical eye over the result and destroy the inferior pieces.

Wood always distorts more in areas of stress, for instance around crotches or knots. If you include a clutch of knots in an otherwise even-grained bowl, you will get more distortion in that area. So the Tasmanian myrtle bowl at right in the photo above was always likely to shrink more on the burry side, causing the form to tilt in that direction. Having a flattish rim, rather than one tapering to a thin edge, emphasizes the distortion. I frequently use beads or grooves for the same purpose. I had hoped that the oak pot, left, would distort and crinkle the beads more than it did. It was cut from near quartersawn wood, so it is oval viewed from above.

If the growth rings are aligned at an angle across the blank, as in the pots in the photo below left, the forms slump to one side. It's not always a bad outcome. Here the pot to the left has the weight low in the form, so it is rather pot-bellied and full of character. The low bulk keeps the form standing firmly both visually and literally. It looks content, even Buddha-like. The top-heavy vessel to the right has warped in the same manner, but here the weight of the dark, denser heartwood at the top has the form off-balance, again both visually and physically; this vessel wants to tip over.

Contrast these forms with those in the photo top right. On the left the end grain again slants across the form, but the light sapwood is on top, with the fullness of the profile, the darker coloring and the weight all low. It looks good and feels fine in the hand. The vertical end grain on the taller vessel indicates that it is quartersawn, confirmed by the sapwood to the left and the pith to the right. This vessel is slightly oval, the wood having shrunk across the grain. Notice how the top has stayed flat, whereas in the other vessels, where the end grain is angled across the form, each rim tilted as the form dried.

The outflowing forms in the photo center right have also warped asymmetrically because the grain was not balanced in the blank. On the left bowl, the pith is to the right of center, so the whole form has lurched in that direction, as the left side shrank more than the right. Had it gone any further, it would have been unstable as well as rather ugly. On the right bowl the growth rings are near vertical; the paler sapwood shrank more than the heartwood on the left. This pulled the form in that direction, tightening the curve, but it did little to improve the rather dumpy shape.

Much better are the bowls in the photo bottom right. Here the foot is smaller in relation to the diameter, creating a more generous, graceful form. The growth rings are seen looping across the profile at about 45 degrees. Greater shrinkage in the paler sapwood has distorted the form just enough to make for an interesting tilt, but not enough to make it unstable.

▲ Pin oak, 5½ in. by 4⅞ in. (140mm × 125mm) and 8¼ in. by 6⅞ in. (210mm × 175mm).

▲ Not all distortion is aesthetically pleasing. Having the pith off-center to the right in the footed bowl caused it to lurch that way. The bowl on the right suffered from having two densities of wood, the lighter sapwood shrinking more than the darker, denser heartwood. Had this bowl been all sapwood or all heartwood, with the vertical growth rings, it would have gone more evenly oval and with the rim remaining flat.

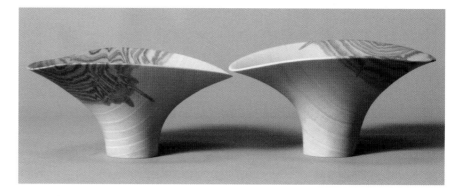

▲ Chinese elm, each 6½ in. (165mm) in diameter.

— 6 —
SURFACE DECORATION
Detailing, Coloring, Burning, Sandblasting

THIS CHAPTER IS ABOUT SURFACES and the details or textures that can be used to add interest to your bowls. Time was when just about all bowl turners were appalled by the notion of coloring wood, let alone painting it. If you wanted decoration, you used beads and grooves, and that was it. Times have changed, and today many turners are exploring ways in which surfaces can be charred, stained, waxed, painted, eroded, and chip-carved, as well as covered with more conventional turned grooves or beads.

When we first discover a technique, it's easy to overuse it. Novice turners who learn to cut beads often cannot resist covering every surface with beads, usually in combination with their new-found cove-cutting ability. We all go through this stage, and our bowls can easily become pretty gross. You need to push on to a better result, turning away excess beads, removing too much paint, and so on, until you have something you can live with. When experimenting, it's the journey and exploration that's exciting, not necessarily the destination. The trick is knowing when to stop. And you'll learn that only by going too far, or up the wrong road.

Most woodturners like to get a head start on the design process by working with highly figured or colorful wood. But as I've warned

▲ Traditionally, turners decorated their bowls with beads and grooves that long outlast the striking color variations of any wood.

◀ Terry Baker decorated the wide rims of these bowls using metal leaf and paint (left), stain and rubbed gold over carving (center), and anti-rust paints (right).

before, don't rely on extravagant color or grain to carry your work indefinitely. Your bowls might look terrific for a few months, maybe years. But unless they're protected from light, air, and use, any one of these will cause the wood to mellow or darken. A few years on a shelf will usually render all but the strongest grain patterns barely discernable. The spectacular and unusual bird's-eye figure in the bowl at the front of the photo above continues to show

◀ ▲ All wood changes color with age. The dark spalting on the sassafras bowl at left, now barely discernable, was initially more contrasting than the spalting on Bill Luce's three Chilean pine bowls shown above. Never rely on grain or spectacular spalting to carry your bowl forever—it's the form that lasts.

as the wood mellows with age, and probably always will, as will other figured (fiddleback or quilted) woods. But it is nothing like as bright as it was when I finished it five years previously.

Less likely to survive is the spectacular dark spalting that splashes across Bill Luce's "Chilean Pine Bowl Set" in the photo at top. Predictably, this will all but vanish, as the lighter wood darkens with exposure to light. Or years of use might bleach the wood to uniformity. Either way, I would anticipate that in a few years the dark and light will blend, much as the heartwood and sapwood in the blackheart sassafras bowl in the photo above. (Twenty years ago this bowl started out the color of those in the photos on page 32.)

To reiterate: the bright color you highlight when finishing wood always fades; therefore, it is essential that your bowls be well formed, so that when the colors do fade, the keepers of your bowls will want to retain them rather than toss them out.

So many woods are a treat to work but lack dramatic grain. Most commercial hardwoods fall into this category. Furniture hardwoods are prized for their working properties. Oak, ash, elm, mahogany, cherry, jarrah, and many other woods are renowned for their ability to take detail. Most mahoganies, for example, work well and hold detailed beading and crisp edges, but mahogany is basically dull. Like so many woods, it is pale when freshly turned, and soon mellows with exposure to light to a deep reddish brown unless stained or French-polished. It would be a pity to avoid such a wonderful material, which can provide the perfect medium for expressing form.

But without a grain pattern or decorative detail to break the surface, even the most ele-

When experimenting, it's the journey and exploration that's exciting, not necessarily the destination.

▲ Transforming wood to look like another material, here using verdigris and gold paint, is not that difficult. And painting is so peaceful after the noise and dust of turning. Note how the three beads serve to link the foot and bowl, the larger piled on top of the smaller so the eye is led from the foot upward and outward. The inset bead below the rim provides an edge to the gold.

gant form tends to be too stark for most people. A well-placed line or bit of texture, as in the serviceable bowl pictured below right, is often just what's needed for visual interest. Such decoration can easily become a signature that defines the work as yours, provided you don't think about it too much and rather let it emerge from the way you handle your tools. Your personal style will soon develop unless too rigorously controlled.

If the wood is really lacklustre, you can obscure the surface entirely and transform your bowl so that nobody has a clue what material it's made from until they handle it, and maybe not even then.

Turned Decoration

On a profile or even inside a bowl, beads and grooves can be used to break up a form horizontally or to emphasize a rim or foot, as in the bowls pictured on this page. On rims pairs of beads or grooves can be used to contain a

▲ This is one of several signature friezes used by Benoît Averly to decorate his simple utilitarian bowls.

▲ Well defined grooves provide an edge to patterns and create a frieze. Andrew Potocnik.

▲ Using meticulously spaced grooves, Bill Luce brings a serenity to this cherry bowl. A touch of black nicely defines the inward tilting rim.

frieze as in the photo above, or provide a sharp edge to bands of paint or gold leaf, as pictured on page 114.

Of the two, grooves are quickest and easiest to turn, as they can be made using a spear-point scraper. Grooves have much the same impact as beads, which is worth noting if you are in business as a production turner. One or two grooves can highlight a rim; more can transform the character of a form. On his cherry bowl, photo left, Bill Luce placed thin grooves with extreme care. The grooves are identical, evenly spaced, and cut cleanly enough to catch the light and create well-defined shadows. These lines might have floated down like particles forming a sedimentary rock in an ancient ocean, making for a serene composition. They also make the bowl less likely to slip from your hands when you pick it up. If lines are used all the way up the profile, they look best when spaced evenly or in some regular progression.

In my looser variations (as in the photos on the facing page) I have a wide band just below

each rim that allows me more margin for error when hollowing. Losing a small amount of width from this band is then no big deal, whereas on Bill Luce's bowl (photo bottom left on the facing page) a thinner band at the rim would detract from the quiet precision of his bowl's profile.

In the photo at right the grooves on the outer bowls were both turned using a thread-chasing tool to cut sets of grooves. Where I maintained space between the sets, left, I was able to ease the chasing tool well into the surface so the grooves are slightly sunken, and this emphasizes the distortion on the completed bowl, pictured above. Having the sets of grooves adjoining, right in the photo at right, requires a light touch, and my intention initially was to have even grooves that formed an evenly textured surface. However, the start of each cut was a shade heavier than required, and it's easy to discern that these are sets of grooves rather than individuals close together. I like the rhythm of the pattern and continue to be happy with the result.

▲▲ None of the sets of beads and grooves that decorate these exteriors go to the rim. Leaving a plain band above and below the grooves allows you to trim both rim and base without messing up the grooves between.

▲ Mike Scott created this 8⅝-in.- (220mm) diameter bowl from a rough chunk of partly seasoned oak, c. 1990. The undercut rim brings a bit of mystery to the inside. To get the color variation on the top, the grooves and rim were charred with a gas torch before being sanded back and polished.

▲ These grooves and beads are simultaneously decorative and functional, providing a groove in which to locate chuck jaws so the bowl can be hollowed, gripping without leaving a mark.

On the 8⅝-in.- (220mm) diameter bowl created from a rough chunk of partly seasoned oak, photo at the top of the facing page, Mike Scott's use of grooves is more textural, especially on the cylindrical inner lip. Both sets of grooves contrast nicely with the rim that is the retained surface of the board from which the blank was cut. Another set of very fine grooves is out of sight on the rounded base.

On outflowing forms like those at bottom left in the photo at the bottom of the facing page, I use grooves that are simultaneously decorative and practical, in that they locate the chuck jaws as the bowl is hollowed. If the groove is on exactly the right diameter for the chuck, the jaws will not mark the wood. Typically, I'll have three grooves, mainly to provide a margin for error, but also because one looks a bit lonely. In fact, each of the bowls in this photo was held in the Shark Jaws of my Vicmarc chuck for hollowing. The jaws closed around the lower bead, top left; the upper bead, top right; and around the lower step, bottom right, in each case without damaging the wood.

In many of the profile drawings in Chapter 3, you will have noticed the use of beads or coves at points of transition, perhaps where the bowl wall meets the foot, or where the rim flares out from the wall. Beads and coves are useful links wherever a profile changes direction, as in the photo at the top of page 117. Beads are used to soften otherwise harsh angles and as a transition between two adjacent surfaces, as in that between the rim and hollow in the photo at right.

If you're not too confident turning beads, use only one or two; then they can be whatever size and shape you like or can live with. If you have three or more, they need regularity and balance. Three can be stacked in order, as above the foot on the bowl top right in the photo at the bottom of the facing page, or with one between a matching pair. Beads covering a larger area, like those top left in this photo, can be the same size, or start small and gradually get larger like ripples in a pond, as at center in the photo at the bottom of page 119. These were turned using a ⅜-in. (9mm) detail gouge, starting with the small beads near the base.

An inset bead like that in the photo at the top of page 117 is simple to turn, being not much more than a pair of grooves with the center rounded over. It's an effective detail that looks more complicated than it is.

Beads that sit on a surface are a different matter and more difficult to get looking good. Beads on a surface look best when the surface on which they sit flows smoothly beneath, as to the right and front in the photo on page 115. It's as if the beads have been applied afterwards, which is the fact with the ebonized bead in the photo below. This bead sits on the inner lip, its blackness defining the inner space and matching the legs. The contrast will survive, though less starkly, even as the maple mellows toward gold. (See also the photo at the top of page 157.)

▼ The ebonized ring is turned separately and set into a recess on the inner lip to provide a stylish rim that complements the matching legs. The rim is veneered MDF for stability, the bowl maple. Made by Andrew Potocnik.

▲ These beads, cut freehand using a ³⁄₈-in. (9mm) detail gouge, feel great in the hand and contrast nicely with the smooth surface into the rim. Turned green, this pot was ebonized and heavily buffed to produce an antique look.

▲ The steps on the profile of this 13¾-in.- (350mm) diameter claret ash fruit bowl were cut into a refined curve. This feature makes lifting a heavy bowl easier than if the profile were smooth.

I particularly enjoy the contrast between beaded curves and smoother surfaces. These can be cut with a special bead-cutting tool, so they are all exactly the same, but I prefer the greater energy imparted to a form when the beads are cut less precisely using a detail gouge. The profile curve is established first, then the beads are cut into that curve, as in the photo at left.

The steps on the profile of the photo below left were similarly cut into a refined curve. The steps are smaller toward the base, as with the lower right bowl in the bottom photo on page 120, only reversed. This detail is highly practical on a large utilitarian bowl because the steps make it easier to lift.

Adding Color

There is a long tradition of coloring turned wood bowls using stains and dyes, although the very thought remains an anathema to many turners. For centuries in Japan most utilitarian turned bowls have been lacquered, I suspect in part because the wood available was not that easy to cut cleanly. Lacquer initially fills the grain, after which it is built up in layers to hide the wood beneath. Lacquering has become an art form in its own right. The elm salad bowl in the photo at the top of the facing page has a finish that imitates a traditional Japanese lacquer finish using anti-rust paint. The profile was painted black in thick, random strokes with a wide brush. The red was sprayed over the black, then rubbed back with wet/dry abrasive to reveal some of the black. Terry Baker applied this same finish to the outside of another of my bowls in 1983. Only after twenty-two years of daily use as a serving and salad bowl did the finish develop a few hairline cracks. It remains in use, washed in hot water and detergent at least six times a week.

The nearest I get to this in my own finishing is in pots like that in the photos at the bottom of the facing page, where you can see

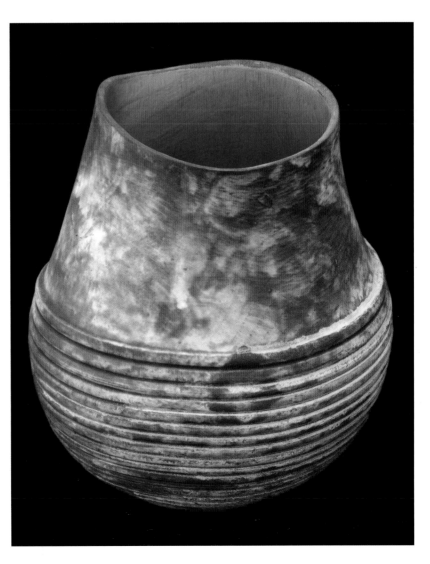

△ Inspired by Japanese lacquerware, this elm salad bowl is finished with tough anti-rust paint. The underlying black was applied thick with broad brush strokes that have been revealed as the sprayed coat of red was initially sanded back, and is now being worn back through use.

the transformation. This bluish verdigris finish is a two-part finish. First, you apply a blackish paint containing copper; when that has dried, a light acid wash brings out the color. Finishes like this, including a rust variation, are found in art- and picture frame–supply stores. The inside is painted with acrylic.

Color can be used effectively to highlight grooves or beads, and you see the difference comparing Andrew Potocnik's small bowls in

△▶ Oak Pot, 6⅜ in. (160mm) in diameter. I liked this pot as it was, but couldn't resist transforming it into a pseudo copper vessel. The truth, however, is evident, as the grain remains visible through the verdigris.

▲ ▲ Whitening the small coves on the profile and simplifying the charred rim, Andrew Potocnik offers a more sophisticated version of the basic form.

the photos above. In the lower one, after the coves are turned on the profile, they are painted with acrylic. When this has dried, the profile is sanded enough that the wood shows through, as the points between each cove are flattened. A similar technique is used for rims like that in the photo top right on the facing page. Patterns speedily carved using a small rotary-ball cutter are painted with acrylic or stained, then the top is sanded back to clear wood, leaving pigment in the incisions. The surface is usually sealed with clear lacquer.

Terry Baker painted my ash bowl in the photo at the top left of the facing page pink, then used a ball grinder to dot into the wood. The small craters are painted with white

acrylic, so the contrast against the pink is maintained as the bowl ages.

Tim Skilton uses crackle paint to decorate his platter rims, center photo on the facing page. Crackle paints, available in a range of colors from art and craft stores, are designed to craze. By applying the paint carefully and varying its thickness, Skilton can consistently control the way the paint cracks. The ring he obtains within the crackle has become a personal detail that sets his platters apart from imitators. After the crackle has dried, he seals it with clear lacquer. To achieve crisp edges to the color, the bowl goes back on the lathe (after the lacquer has dried) to complete turning and finishing.

A bewildering array of paints and pastes in modern art-supply stores enable you to color and texture just about any material (see also the photo on page 114). Using acrylic texture paste, Liz Scobie builds layers of texture on her husband Neil's bowls, one of which appears in the photo at the bottom of the facing page. Liz Scobie adds a small amount of pigment to the paste prior to application to provide a base color. Once that's dry, she builds layers of acrylic color on top. She prefers to paint fine lines with a brush, but fiber-tipped tools are an alternative.

Texture paste is a wonderful medium. It's white, thick enough to be shaped and molded, and tough enough to be peaked like frosting on a cake and withstand a few gentle knocks. You can color it with acrylic or water-based

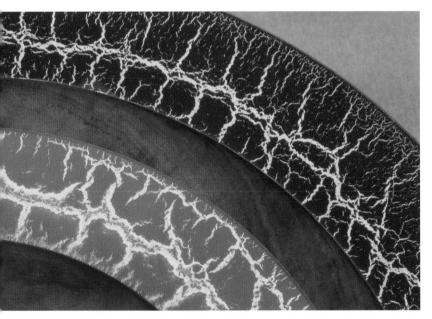

◀ Terrry Baker used a ball grinder and
acrylic paint to dress up this beaded bowl,
which I turned from ash.

▲ Andrew Potocnik painted this carved rim
then sanded back the high-lines to the wood, so
the pigment accentuates the carving. Random
patterns like this look better bordered by a thin
black groove or a wider, untextured band.

◀ Tim Skilton controls crackle paint to create
his signature effect in the 2-in.- (50mm) wide
rims on his 16-in.- to 20-in.- (400mm to
500mm) diameter platters.

▼ Using acrylic paints over texture paste,
Liz Scobie added to the basic form, turned
and carved by husband Neil, to complete this
"Nautelous Bowl." The texture is all paste
and paint, not carving into the wood.

▲▲ Bill Luce used black dye and bleach to transform these black locust and maple bowls; both have sand-etched outsides that contrast with smooth interiors. Note how the well-defined black locust growth rings have been carefully aligned to lie parallel to the rim and surface on which the bowl sits, whereas the maple surface might have been rendered with coarse cement trowelled on at random. Each is timeless.

paints, or bulk it out with fine shavings, sawdust, or even sand. When it's dry, you can cut into it, scratch it, or paint it. The paste can be applied with knives or brushes.

Dyes penetrate the wood more than paint, which adheres to the surface. The advantage of dye is that it will penetrate deep into corners and crevices, so it is a good way to change the color of a surface like the highly etched open grain of Bill Luce's black honeylocust bowl in the photo at left. If you don't like the thought of color, bleach acts in much the same way but giving you a surface like that on driftwood, as in the photo below left.

If a stained surface is sanded back, it becomes progressively paler, with the remnants of the stain finally only in the pores, which highlights the growth rings in ring-porous woods like the claret ash in the photo at bottom left on the facing page.

On a smoother surface I used a wax-resist technique employed by potters in their brush decorations, photo bottom right on the facing page. Designs and patterns are painted using hot wax that sets as it contacts the cooler wood. Then the bowl is soaked in a vat of dye, in this case indigo, for an hour, during which time the dye stains the wood everywhere except the waxed areas. After the bowl is dry, it goes back on the lathe to be polished, and because there is so much wax on it, all you need do is apply a rag to the spinning wood to melt the wax and spread it across the whole bowl. Such bowls can look very ceramic from a distance.

Another way of coloring wood is using colored wax. Wax containing lime (calcium oxide) has long been used to highlight the grain on dark woods with large pores, and particularly on oak furniture. The oak bowl, left in the photo at top on the facing page, was lime-waxed after it was stained with the rusty-nails-and-vinegar mix. As you can see, the white lime lodged in the open pores but not in the dense rays that swirl across the bands of

TANNIN-REACTIVE EBONIZING

When tannin occurs in a wood, as it does in the oak and Tasmanian myrtle bowls in the photo at right, the wood can be stained black—or ebonized (that is, made to look like ebony)—using a brew that reacts with the tannin. In a glass jar filled with vinegar soak odd bits of old iron like rusty washers, nuts and bolts, iron filings, or the metal particles beneath your grinder. In a day or so the vinegar goes a very dark blue with a scummy, frothy top. Paint this on wood containing tannin, and the surface goes black within a few minutes. The vinegar ferments, so never fix a lid on the container, or it may explode.

You will quickly discover if unseasoned wood contains much tannin because it stains your hands black as you turn it. (Lemon juice removes the stain.) And because tannin reacts with iron, contact with ferrous metal like steel chuck jaws will induce a dark blue-to-purple stain on the wood. I have had rough-turned bowls speckled by sparks from the grinder when sharpening tools, but it was not a finish that appealed to me so I've not pursued it. (If you come across a patch of such color in a log, you can expect to find a nail or larger chunk of iron close by.)

Woods containing tannin can also be darkened by fuming with ammonia in a small enclosed space. The simplest way to fume a bowl is to seal it inside a tent made from a plastic bag, along with an open container holding about two cups of

▲ The oak bowl, left, was ebonized then lime-waxed. The white lime lodged in the open pores of the growth rings but not in the dense rays that swirl across these bands. The Tasmanian myrtle, right, was ebonized to a denser black. It was then buffed on a high-speed buffing wheel until the high spots were cut back to the underlying wood, producing a patina associated with long use.

ammonia. Household ammonia will work, but more concentrated (and expensive) ammonia you can buy at a pharmacy is better. Fuming periods vary considerably, depending on the wood and how dark you want it. I figure two weeks maximum, but check the color daily. The gases must be able to circulate freely around the wood, so construct a simple box in the bag or erect a tripod of small sticks, like a tepee. In either case, secure the bag so that fumes cannot escape. And don't forget to hold your breath when you open it—the

fumes are not pleasant or healthy.

If you rest the bowl on its base, the bottom will not change color because the gases cannot reach the wood's surface; if you rest the bowl on its rim, you can fume the outside without affecting the interior. So initially you can have color variations, but these are soon nullified by light and air. Fuming merely speeds up the natural process of aging, although there is a bonus in that the sanded surface of many woods feels much smoother, almost silky, after fuming.

▲ These ash bowls were stained an intense blue then sanded back to reveal the wood and highlight the grain.

◄ Wax was daubed on the bare ash before this bowl was dipped in indigo dye. Dye cannot penetrate the waxed areas. When dry, the bowl went back on the lathe to be polished using a soft cloth, which melted the wax, revealing the undyed areas and coating the entire surface evenly.

▲ Non-tarnishing gold, silver, and copper waxes were blended over these 6-in.- to 8-in.- (150mm to 200mm) diameter bowls that had been stained black (bowls on the left), and greenish-blue (right).

▲ Pascal Oudet used an oxyacetylene torch and sandblasting to etch the profile of this 6-in.- (150mm) diameter ash bowl. After a final light charring and layers of Danish oil, the surface becomes almost soft, like old leather. The inside is gold leaf.

white. You can emphasize the pores on pale open-grained woods simply by polishing the bowl as it spins on the lathe with a grubby rag. For a bit of subtle color in the pores, I add a dollop of powder paint (popular in kindergartens) to the oil when I am oiling a bowl. When the bowl is polished, the color that got into the pores remains, while the excess collects on the polishing cloth.

The bowls in the photo at left were finished with non-tarnishing gilt waxes. These are expensive but go a long way. I blended gold, copper, and silver waxes on top of surfaces stained black (the two bowls on the left), and greenish-blue (right). The advantage of colored waxes is that they don't obscure the grain completely. The disadvantage is that in temperatures of over 95°F (35°C) it softens and stains your hands if you handle the bowl.

For many people a more obvious touch of precious metal increases the preciousness of an object. On the pseudo-metal bowl in the photo at the bottom of page 104 a touch of gold highlights the bead that separates the rust and verdigris. This gold is gouache painted on, whereas the golden inside of Pascal Oudet's little round bowl in the photo at left is gold leaf. Terry Baker uses a variegated metal leaf on many of his small production bowls, like that in the photo at the top of the facing page. The ultra thin leaf adheres to size painted on the raw wood, after which it is lacquered. Even though the leaf edge undulates, a groove just below the inner lip defines the lower reaches of the leaf, also deliniating the upper reaches of the dots. The crimson lines were painted over the leaf.

Pyrography

Pyrography, a method of marking wood using a red-hot steel point, is a whole craft industry in itself, much of it to do with carving decoy birds. Pyrographically decorated turned objects have a long tradition in many parts of the world. In Scandinavia and Central and Eastern Europe, turned bowls and platters were

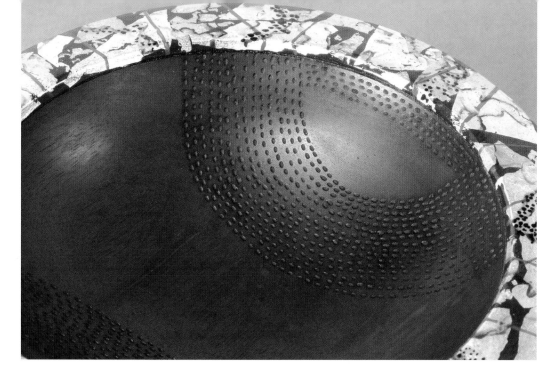

◄ The line below the inner lip serves as a border for both the rim decoration and the pyrographic dot motif below. Red gum, 8-in.- (200mm) diameter. Made by Terry Baker, c. 1990.

◄ Terry Baker's dot patterns, burnt using a hot wire, are a tactile as well as visual enhancement

often adorned with village scenes and geometric patterns. In Australia Terry Baker has developed his own vocabulary based on Aboriginal and tribal art. Using dots burned into the wood, as in the photos above, Baker builds larger patterns that you can feel as well as see. The wood has darkened considerably since this bowl pictured at top was made over ten years ago, but the burnt indentations

remain visible, and of course you can still feel them.

You no longer have to heat up the fireplace poker for pyrography, because these days you can purchase electric pyrographic burners. These consist of a small transformer with a temperature control dial, or rheostat, attached by cable to a pen, which holds a variety of tips. Pyrographic pens work well on close- and

◀ Douglas Bell uses the red-hot wire on a pyrographic pen to burn his drawings into the rims of these 8-in.- (200mm) diameter jacaranda bowls.

▼ Terry Scott used the dividing head on his lathe to lay out the radial lines on which to base the frieze for this 13¾-in. by 3⅜-in. (350mm x 85mm) rimu (*Dacridium cupressinum*) bowl. Note how the pattern is set in a shallow recess and how the inwardly inclined plane forms the inner lip. Even if the wood blackens with age, the incised pattern will remain.

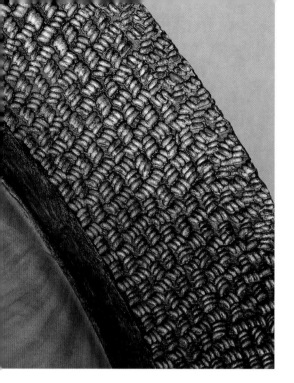

▲ Terry Scott stamped the multitude of triplets that detail this 2³⁄₈-in.- (60mm) wide rim using a brand he made himself by winding his pyrograph's wire into a coil. The inner band is tapa cloth laid over a bead. (For more about tapa cloth, see page 145.)

even-grained woods, and, obviously, the black line stands out best on pale woods. It is not easy to get an even line burnt into uneven surfaces, such as end-grain softwoods with their alternately soft and hard annual rings.

Many woodturners sign their work using a pyrographic pen, so it is no surprise that many use it also for decorating their work. Douglas Bell had almost completed his usual grassy rim, left in the photo at the top of the facing page, when a bumped elbow jammed the hot pen into the outer rim leaving a heavy burn mark. Recognizing a design opportunity, the burn became a bull-rush seed pod that had to be matched by others, and Bell had a new motif, right in the same photo. The background is dotted in last. If you're looking for things to do, coloring in such a design should keep you occupied, and the burned grooves will provide a good edge to contain the color.

Most pyrographic burners now come with a range of tips that make life easier than the old-style loop of hot wire, particularly for straight lines like those that make up the pattern on the rim of Terry Scott's large rimu

(a New Zealand red pine) bowl in the photo at the bottom of the facing page. Straight and even lines are difficult to achieve using a loop end. On another wide rim, photo left, Scott used a helical brand he made by winding his pyrograph's wire around a small nail. To maintain control of this sort of pattern and prevent it creeping around the circle, he finds it best to divide a rim into 24 segments, then use the pyrograph to brand the pattern within those segments. Finally, he brushed the surface with boot polish.

To create black lines like those on the ash bowl in the photo below quickly and easily without resorting to ink or paint or pyrographic pen, you cut a small groove which is then burnt through friction. On the outside of a bowl the preferred method is to pull a length of strong wire, such as piano wire, into a narrow groove until you get smoke and a black line. Wires for this purpose are available through woodturning supply stores, or you can make your own by attaching a good-sized knob to each end of 12 in. (305mm) or so of wire. Alternatively, cut a thin—say, ¹⁄₁₆-in. (2mm)—hardwood batten, and push this into the groove until there's smoke and the groove is charred. A 1-in.-wide wood batten will vanish into smoke, marking a ring on a medium-sized bowl.

▼ Grooves can be charred simply by holding a taut wire or slim batten in the groove as the wood spins on the lathe. Friction builds enough heat to char the wood. For crisp definition of the blackened grooves, sand after the charring.

Burning, Sandblasting, and Brushing

This chapter and the next include a number of images of bowls whose surfaces have been eroded by sandblasting, wire brushes, or flame. Combined with other techniques, the decorative and tactile possibilities of these surfaces are limitless.

Pyromaniacs will be delighted to know that whole bowls can be charred and etched using a gas torch. Oxyacetylene burns faster and deeper than propane, which is the most commonly used fuel. When the surface is thoroughly burned, the loose char is brushed or sandblasted off. To fake a patina of age, Terry Baker repeated this process several times using a propane torch on his large "Celtic Series" bowl in the photos above and left.

The outside of Pascal Oudet's 6-in. (150mm) ash bowl (photo at the bottom of page 128) was more aggressively burnt with an oxyacetylene blowtorch, then sandblasted three times. The surface was scorched once more, and the resulting soot removed with a soft brush. The outside is finished with multiple coats of Danish oil.

Much the same technique was used on the square oak bowl in the photo at the top of the facing page, except that the charred surface was attacked with a steel-wire brush set in an elec-

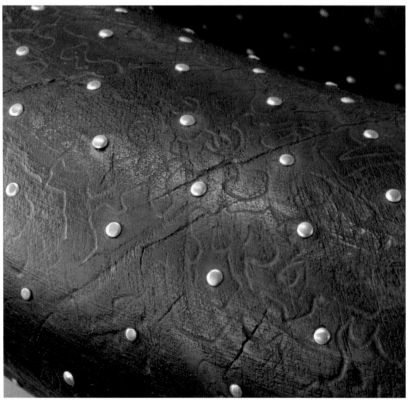

▲▲ Terry Baker's work is often characterised by the use of dots. (In his bowl on page 125 the dots are carved with a ball grinder then painted with white acrylic; in his bowls on page 129 the dots are burnt using a hot wire.) The surface on this 23-in.- (585mm) diameter jarrah "Celtic Series" bowl is heavily carved using a Dremel burr, then charred using a gas torch, sanded back, and reworked again to create a very subtle surface from which all manner of patterns emerge. The pins are laid out on a grid and glued into drilled holes.

◀ This oak bowl was very heavily scorched, and aggressively brushed with a wire wheel brush mounted in a high-speed drill to produce the undulating surface. After another lighter charring, I finally brushed it using a soft Nylox abrasive nylon brush, then finished with boiled linseed oil.

▼ Andrew Potocnik retained the silvery weathered exterior of the red gum log that contrasts nicely with the red interior as well as the black outside.

tric drill—a particularly messy operation requiring good dust extraction. I keep the bowl on the lathe for convenience, but with the spindle locked so I can take the rotating brush to the wood. I keep the brush rotating parallel to the grain, so there are no scratches across the ridges, and finish the surface using a Nylox abrasive nylon wheel brush. This bowl was a very rough and gutsy bit of turning using a partly seasoned more-or-less square block of pin oak. I'd hoped it would split somewhat before I burnt it, but it didn't, nor did it warp much. My intention was to create a bowl that looked as though it had had a hard life for centuries and might have come out of some peat bog.

With similar intentions, Andrew Potocnik roughed the outside of his round-bottomed bowl in the photo center left before eroding the surface with flame and brush. Potocnik retained the silvery weathered outside of the red gum log, which contrasts nicely with the natural red of the interior as well as the charred outside.

More refined is the exterior surface of the 13-in.- (330mm) diameter elm bowl in the photo bottom left. With the lathe spinning slowly at about 400 rpm, I used a drill-mounted wire brush to etch away the softer grain of the turned (but not sanded) outside. I charred this lightly before brushing it with a soft Nylox wheel brush.

▲ Although etched, the black profile of this 13-in.- (330mm) diameter elm bowl feels soft as it surrounds the glowing inside.

▲ I usually deal with an intrusive knot or split by charring it with a gas torch, then sanding away the black almost to clean wood using drill-mounted Nylox abrasive nylon brushes.

▲ Turned green, this Tasmanian oak burl split badly as it dried. With nothing to lose, I sandblasted it to clean away torn fibers that hung across the cracks. It would have made a fine colander, but has been used in the kitchen to store potatoes and onions for at least twenty years.

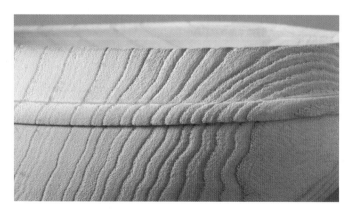

▲ Sandblasting highlights the grain patterns as it etches the surface. As seen in many images in this book, this surface can be stained or bleached, as in the photos on page 126, or burned and brushed, as in the photo at the bottom of page 128.

Selective burning with a gas torch is also a good way to deal with intrusive knots, like that in the photo at left, or splits. This bowl was an experiment in turning a heavy form from freshly felled oak. It is a uniform 2 in. (50mm) thick and warped only slightly, as expected. The very dense, short-grained, and consequently brittle wood on the ingrown knot chipped as it was turned. I broke away as much as possible, to get down to solid wood, and burnt the surface smooth, then sanded it back using the Nylox brushes. On many woods (but not here) heat will cause the wood to split, particularly on the end grain; such splits can be detailed in much the same way.

Sandblasting is the best way to remove soft areas of grain to produce a weathered effect as in the two lower photos at left. The abrasive sand cleans out any splits and in a few seconds most woods look as though they've been out in all weathers for years. Don't expect the process to eliminate signs of poor workmanship; it is more likely to highlight them. Surfaces must be well finished, because any scratch will be worn down evenly along with the surface it scars. The best results usually come from wood with a pronounced difference between the hard latewood and the soft earlywood of the growth rings.

If you don't have space for, or cannot justify, your own small sandblaster, you should find at least one abrasive blasting business in your Yellow Pages, the sort of operation that cleans and etches all manner of materials.

You can remove a good deal of soft wood using a simple wire brush held against the spinning wood. The only problem is that this also creates concentric scratch marks. More effective is a wire wheel brush mounted in a drill—the technique I used on the elm bowl in the photo at the bottom of page 133 prior to charring it. Rotated directly against the oncoming wood, the brush will tear out the softer wood much faster, but still leave concentric lines. Held at an angle, the brush will leave swirling lines.

DON'T OVERDO IT

Limited use of decoration can do wonders for a bowl. But resist the temptation to smother a bowl with all manner of decorative tricks; restraint is the key to success. While I enjoy exploring ways of combining a range of differing techniques, I still find most satisfying the subtleties and unique character of a cleanly cut surface.

The miniscule spiral groove left by a gouge on the silky oak bowl in the photo at right is barely discernable. It's best seen just below the grooves, then less so further down. Clearly, the grooves were cut using a spear-point scraper and could have been cut a lot cleaner. My defense is that these grooves are barely 3/32 in. (2mm) wide, so you need pretty good eyesight to spot the quality of the cut, even at its poorest, here on the end grain. The surface on this profile is unobtainable using abrasives, but it is my sad experience that a good finish straight from the tool is virtually unmarketable. It's not rough enough for the hair-shirt brigade, nor smooth enough for the jet set (and I suppose not shiny enough for the masses in between). As a result, I leave very few bowls this way, which is a pity because the subtle marks of skillful tool handling can greatly enhance an object's appeal. And it's an achievement you can justifiably feel smug about too.

The subtle marks of skillful tool handling can greatly enhance on object's appeal.

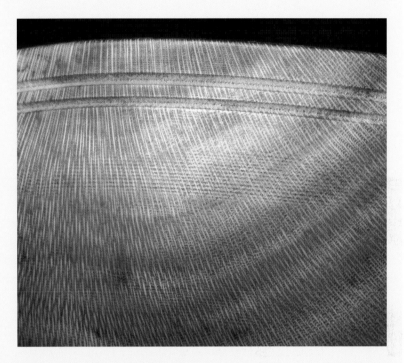

A fine spiral that results from a clean cut with a gouge is difficult to beat.

Wavy oak bowls, 11 in. and 8 in. (280mm and 200mm) in diameter.

— 7 —

DECORATIVE RESHAPING

Carved, Pierced, Hacked, Hewed, and Joined

I N THIS CHAPTER YOU'LL SEE HOW CARVING, piercing, and cutting can be used to create decorative patterns on bowls, as well as more free-form sculpted and constructed pieces. So often a turned form is simply not satisfying enough, especially when the wood is somewhat bland, devoid of strong figure and color. Then, for some, the plain surface cries out to be decorated, perhaps as does a white wall to a vandal bent on graffiti. If, in our world of labor-saving devices, we had the free time enjoyed by the so-called primitive societies of the past, we might fill it by quietly decorating all our bowls with carving.

However, no longer do carvers use only simple, traditional carving tools and occasionally a mallet. Today numerous power tools on the market enable us to change the shape of wood very quickly, though often with a great deal of noise and dust. Power-carving burrs and cutters come in a wide range of shapes and sizes. These are easiest to use mounted in a flexible drive shaft with a variable-speed motor, and are available through specialist woodcarving and woodturning catalogs. These cutters can also be mounted in small rotary tools, the best known of which is the Dremel. These tools are ideal for fine work on a small scale. For larger projects, where a great deal of

▲ A stained-black exterior and gold-leaf interior highlight this filigree detail of a vessel pictured on page 151.

◄ Bowls don't come much better than this fine 13¾-in. (350mm) fumed oak pot by Liam Flynn.

wood is to be removed, power-carving chisels with interchangeable blades of various shapes are more suitable. In addition, Arbortech rotary carvers and their clones fit on to angle grinders. For smoother surfaces a wide range of power sanding disks, wheels, and cylinders attach to electric drills. It's a tool-junkie's heaven out there.

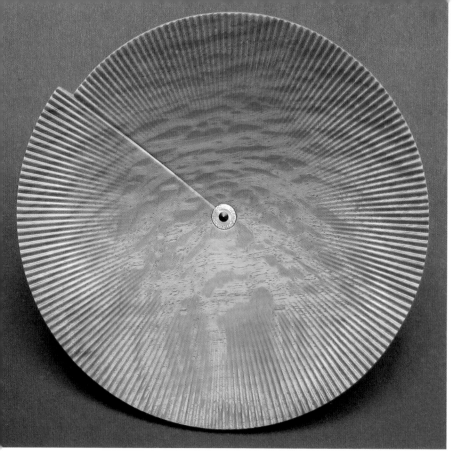

▲ "Fluted Bowl," by Vaughn Richmond, she-oak, 6 in. by 2 in (150mm × 50mm). The stud in the center is hand-cast pewter with an insert of pearl-shell and kelp (as in seaweed), all turned with standard turning tools.

Flutes, Grooves, and Pattern

All the bowls in this section are decorated with grooves, the width and texture of which are largely dictated by the tools used to make them. The subtle variations of freehand work are usually more appealing than similar jig-guided work. On the other hand, very stylish decoration can be created with a jigged router, drill, or chainsaw used in conjunction with the lathe's dividing head. Most lathes have such a head, enabling you to lock the drive spindle (and therefore any job on the lathe) in regu-

The subtle variations of freehand work are usually more appealing than similar jig-guided work.

larly spaced positions to cut radially symmetrical or spiral patterns (see sidebar on page 142).

Hand carving applied to a stunning form produces some of the most sublime wooden bowls ever made, among which would have to be Irishman Liam Flynn's oak bowl in the photo on page 136 with Flynn's signature double rim. The fact that these flutes are carved by hand brings a subtle irregularity to the surface. The ridges between the grooves remain crisp as they wander very slightly, catching the light and creating a set of shadows that give us the shape of the bowl.

Vaughn Richmond's machined and sanded internal flutes in the photo at left are equally contemplative. Richmond set up a router in a jig to cut flutes in from the rim of his she-oak bowl. He comments that the process was painfully slow and extremely noisy, and that sanding each groove was a bit of a challenge! Nevertheless, the sanding produces a nice corrugated effect, softening the precise routing. And that bit of handwork has created flutes that vary in length, so some reach further towards center than others. With the rim cut to create the hint of a spiral that begins and ends at the line that leads to the central stud, the dish looks like an aerial view of a launch pad with a rocket sitting quietly, ready to go, or a hi-tech surveillance dish.

Mike Scott's "Segmented Discus Form," photo at the top of the facing page, is more of an ancient gear wheel, emphasized in this photo by the shadow of the rim. The radial grooves across the top were routed on a straight jig across the curved surface to create the subtle wedges. The bottom of each V is in line; you can put a straight-edge along each one. Burning and brushing etched the grain and softened the edges; then all but the inside was stained black to ensure an even density of color to surround the gold interior that is gouache.

Router cuts kept square bring a different character to a bowl. Fred Morton, an engineer who spends his days dealing with vehicle

transmissions, prefers nice square grooves, reminiscent of gears, photo below left. A series of turned grooves on the outside crosses the routed grooves on the inside to create a lattice. These require careful sanding with abrasive wrapped around a machined block, to avoid rounding over the edges. This work demands flowing curves and a carefully controlled wall thickness, though not necessarily even throughout. Having the wall thicken toward the rim gave Morton enough material to carve the wavy rim in the photo below right. The wide valleys that create the undulating upper profile and rim were machined using a drill-mounted cutter held in a jig that guides the cut straight toward center. The internal slots were routed into the valleys to meet concentric grooves turned on the exterior.

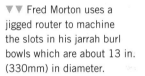

▲ "Segmented Discus Form," by Mike Scott, elm and gold paint 13 in. by 4½ in. (330mm × 115mm).

▼ ▼ Fred Morton uses a jigged router to machine the slots in his jarrah burl bowls which are about 13 in. (330mm) in diameter.

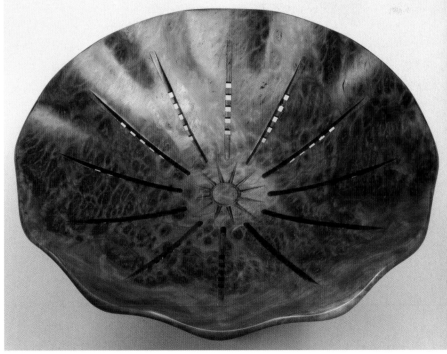

▲ "Ceremonial Vessel" by Mike Scott, c.1995, 31 in. by
12 in. (790mm × 305mm). The antithesis of what so many
turners strive to achieve, with its roughly turned surfaces,
detailed defects, and selective charring, this large elm bowl
exudes raw energy. The big staple looks just right, as though
it's needed, even though it's probably not.

▼ Patterns can come from commercially available
tools. Fred Morton used a Teknatool Nova Ornamental
Turner to cut the interlocking rings, left, and a Sorby
Texturing Tool for the swirling striation, right.

Working on a much larger scale, Mike Scott uses an electric chainsaw mounted on a sliding pivot to cut out grooves on his monumental works. His "Ceremonial Bowl," photo at the top of the facing page, is the antithesis of what so many turners strive to achieve; with its roughly turned surfaces, detailed defects, and selective charring, this bowl exudes raw energy. The big staple looks just right, as though it's needed, even though it's probably not.

In decorating the rims of the bowls in the photo at the bottom of the facing page, Fred Morton used a Teknatool Nova Ornamental Turner to cut the interlocking rings, left, and a Sorby Texturing Tool for the swirling striation, right. The interlocking rings are a very simple form of ornamental turning, an area of woodturning that amounts to a separate craft, involving specialized indexing equipment and mechanized cutters to create a myriad of elaborate and precise geometric patterns. Sorby Texturing Tools are supplied with several heads that produce different patterns and textures, the edges of which are somewhat ragged. To contain the swirling texture, the beads are only blocked out before applying the Texture Tool, then finished when the texturing is completed. Any staining or burning also must be done before completing the beads.

On his very large platter, photo top right, Terry Baker burnt and polished the 3-in.- (75mm) wide rim before chasing radial grooves in it with a Dremel grinder. By working freehand and varying the pressure of the cut, he retained the original surface in flats of varying widths, to contrast with the alternating coves. Light plays across these polished flats and on their undulating edges, making this rim especially interesting to move about.

The oak used for the dish in the photo bottom right is a very pale yellow. To achieve an effect similar to that on the rim in the photo top right, Baker used a hand-held air-driven die grinder with a ¼-in. (6mm) ball to cut

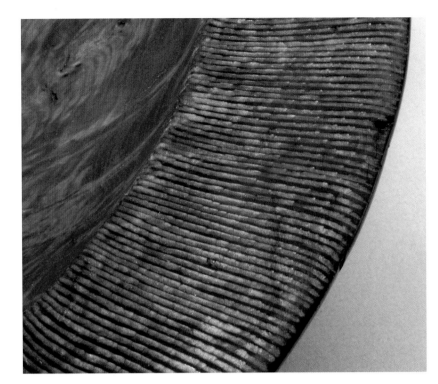

striations, before staining the whole bowl black. He worked the stain well into the grooves using a ½-in. (13mm) brush, thus eliminating the air bubbles that prevent penetration of the color. The bowl went back on the lathe for a light sanding with 240 grit to cut back through the stained surface to the lighter wood beneath. The strong, widely

▲▲ Terry Baker used high-speed ball grinders to decorate these bowls, emphasizing the grooves through charring, top, and stain and sanding, above.

Again using a high-speed ball grinder to create the grooves, Terry Baker here emphasized them with lime paste.

LAYOUT USING THE LATHE

While a bowl is on the lathe, you can lay out a grid from which to develop any number of patterns. First, mark a series of concentric rings ³⁄₁₆ in. (5mm) apart up the profile. Use a sharp HB pencil for accuracy. Next, draw radial lines to divide the surface into equal segments. Most lathes have a dividing head that enables you to do this. Set your T-rest so that your pencil is at center height as you draw the lines. This is most easily done using a flat-topped rest or table against which you can hold the pencil firmly so that, as you draw around the profile, you do so in one plane. It helps to have a collar to support the tool rest, as this allows you to swing the rest around and maintain support for the pencil near the wood without changing height. Once you have an accurate grid, patterns are created by connecting intersections. If your radial lines miss center and lie more toward the tangential, provided they are marked in the same plane, you'll lay out a warped grid that will offer a completely different set of patterns.

spaced annular rings break up the carved striations to create something of a moiré effect, as the pattern appears to shift when you move around it.

Baker used a Dremel cutter to carve the chevron frieze on one of my elm bowls, photo above. The grooves were limed to heighten the contrast with the smoother wood (increasingly dark due to age and use) on the remainder of the bowl.

Again with a high-speed ball, and working loosely freehand on a precise grid, Terry Baker carved the outer squares of his "Celtic Series" dish, photo at the top of the facing page. Next, he softened the pattern using a gas torch and heavy brushing, masking the central square to preserve its precise edge. Then he cut the central square and patterns into the charred surface with the same high-speed ball. The brass pins, glued into pre-drilled holes, highlight the grid.

To incise the much narrower lines on the outside of his large bowl made from rimu, photo at the bottom of the facing page, Terry Scott used a heated knife. He laid out the grid for the design on the lathe beginning with equally spaced concentric rings and adding radial lines at intervals (a division of eight), with the aid of the dividing head. Scott did not find compass-drawn arcs visually satisfactory (the provenance of the ornamental turner), so penciled in the design, then burned in all the lines freehand using a red-hot knife. Finally, he stained the incised area black, adding a touch of rub-on bronze to bring a hint of iridescence to the surface.

◄ Terry Baker erodes heavily carved surfaces by burning with a gas torch and removing the soot with wire rotary brushes, often several times. Finally the surface is sanded with 240-grit abrasive. On this "Celtic Dish" the brass pins were glued into predrilled holes.

◄ Laying it out with the aid of the lathe's dividing head, Terry Scott cut this pattern into the outside of his rimu bowl using a red-hot knife. The iridescence was achieved by adding a touch of rub-on bronze over the black stain.

▲ By varying the width of the carved band on this green-turned 6¾-in.- (170mm) diameter holly bowl, Liam Flynn imposes another dimension on a form already distorted to oval.

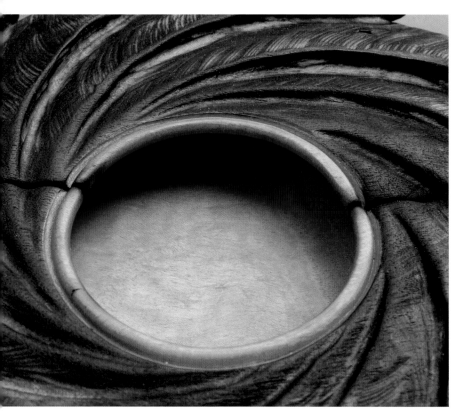

▲ ▶ The cyclonic swirls of Andrew Potocnik's "Razorback" were charred and vigorously brushed back to reveal some splashes of redgum, 8⅝-in. (220mm) diameter.

The much deeper grooves that define the interwoven leaves on the rim of Liam Flynn's small holly bowl, photo at the top of the facing page, were carved with a V-tool, then fluted with a shallow gouge, by hand.

In the photos at the bottom of the facing page Andrew Potocnik used an Arbortech Rotary Woodcarver on its side to create extra texture on the facets of the heavily incised cyclonic spirals of his "Razorback." These were burnt with a propane gas torch held at an angle, so the valleys are less charred. The heavily burned areas remained darkened, while elsewhere brushing has returned natural wood to the surface.

Terry Scott employs a variety of power-carving and sanding tools to carve into the undersides of his large platters (photos at right). The stippled spiral was branded with his homemade branding tool (compare the photo at the top of page 131). Both the carved spiral and the recessed trefoil are inlaid with tapa cloth, a strong fabric pounded from the inner bark of the paper mulberry tree. It is the traditional cloth of the South Pacific. On both bowls the tapa is pasted to the wood, with the edges wedged into a thin groove for a neat finish. The trefoil makes a dramatic base that I was not prepared for when, as a judge for an exhibition, I first handled this bowl. The bowl rests on the three pairs of pale dots at the cusps of the trefoil.

▶▶ Terry Scott inlaid both the carved spiral and recessed trefoil with tapa cloth, a strong fabric pounded from the inner bark of the paper mulberry tree. The traditional cloth of the South Pacific, the tapa is pasted to the wood, with the edges wedged into a thin groove for a neat finish.

▲ Vaughn Richmond made each of the studs for this rim detail by turning an ebony ring to surround a copper tube filled with a mountain ash dowel. The fan is 2⅛ in. (55mm) across the top. Quilted jarrah, 8⅜ in. by 3⅜ in. (210mm × 85mm).

Freehand Carving and Sculpting

Carving can be used to facet a whole surface, as in the photo below right. This exterior was textured using a power-carving tool with a shallow gouge, then stained. All that was needed to highlight the lattice of ridges was a quick rub with a Scotchbrite pad. The purpose of the groove is to provide an edge to the faceted surface, and of course a smooth band at the rim, which looks better than carving all the way to the rim.

Carved details can also add considerable refinement or bring illusion to a form. Vaughn Richmond is known for quiet and restrained detailing. The grooves on the inside of his she-oak bowl, photo below left, appear to be steps that connect the two levels of a spiraling rim. Lowering the height of the rim at the end of the grooves creates the illusion that this bowl might be somehow wrapped into a cone. On a similar small bowl, photo at left, Richmond carved a spine into the bowl that

▲ The three flutes and barely spiralled rim create an optical illusion on this 12¼-in. by 4½-in. (310mm × 115mm) she-oak bowl. "Groovy," Vaughan Richmond.

▼ The groove provides a well defined edge to the carving. After the black stain dried, the carved surface was rubbed with a Scotchbrite pad to create the lattice of pale lines that define the facets.

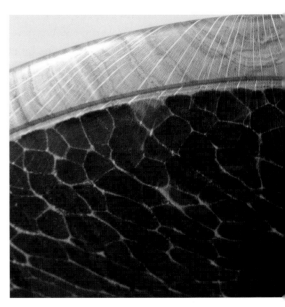

▲▼▼ Cutting a pair of spirals into a rim enables me to rescue many thin bowls that split. The technique works best on steeper profiles. Open bowls appear elongated from above and anything but round, which they still are.

develops from the sides of the 2-in.- (50mm) wide studded and stippled fan-shaped detail. Note how the left side flows up into the end of the spiral on the rim that started at the corner on the right, just as on the fluted bowl pictured below it. The studs are turned separately, each made up of an ebony ring surrounding a copper tube filled with a mountain ash dowel.

Shaping the rim into a pair of complementary spiral arcs is how I deal with bowls that have a split on the rim, usually from the pith. With the bowl on its side, I bandsaw in on the split, and make a matching cut opposite. Then I saw from the top of each cut to the bottom of the other and sand. I do this to rescue split bowls that I would otherwise have to reduce in height or even throw out. By retaining the maximum dimensions of the original bowl, I don't need to reduce the price; rather it goes up! This technique works best on steep profiles, as in the cherry bowl in the photo above. More out-flowing forms, like that in the photo center right, tend to look elongated, and even unbalanced if the grain pattern is strong. To cope with splits in the green-turned holly bowl, upper right in the photo bottom right, I simply curved the rim into the bottom of the split.

▲ "The Future is Functional," by Art Liestman, curly cherry and ebony. 7½ in. by 3 in. (190mm × 75mm).

◄ ▼ When a rim is carved, like these from Neil Scobie, it is essential that the internal curves flow smoothly and are free of any dips or bumps that would mar the line of the inner lip of the rim. At left, "Wave Rim," red cedar, 15¾ in. by 4⅞ in. (400mm × 125mm); and below, "Huon Erosion," huon pine, 7¼ in. by 2¾ in. (185mm × 70mm).

Once you overcome your fear of possibly wrecking your bowl, cutting into a rim has endless possibilities.

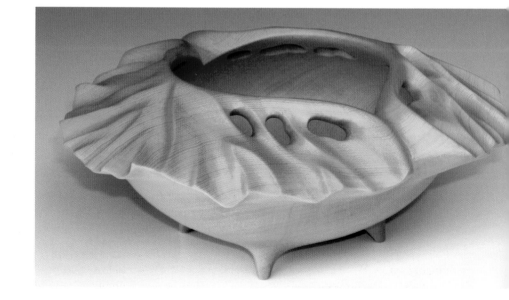

▲ *"Qui s'y frotte"* (You Might Get Stung), by Pascal Oudet, rowan, 7 in. (180mm) in diameter, 3/16 in. (5mm) thick.

Those less commercially oriented can be more frivolous, like Art Liestman with the rim of his jigsaw bowl, photo at top of the facing page. Once you overcome the fear of possibly wrecking your bowl, cutting into a rim has endless possibilities. If you keep the high points of the rim in one horizontal plane, and the low points in another—so each plane is parallel to the table the bowl sits on—your bowls will usually look better balanced.

Neil Scobie turns simple forms with big fat rims that he can carve. Inspired by coastal scenery, Scobie's rims—like those on his two bowls pictured on the facing page: his large Australian red cedar bowl "Wave Rim" and smaller "Huon Erosion"—are reminiscent of sand and rock sculpted by wind and water. The only hint of the original turned rim on the cedar bowl is seen near the end of the upswinging wings. For this sort of work, it is essential that the internal curves flow

smoothly, and are free of any dips or bumps that would mar the line of the inner lip of the rim.

To achieve his spikey little *"Qui s'y frotte"* (You Might Get Stung) natural-edge rowan (mountain ash) bowl, photo above, Frenchman Pascal Oudet overcame several challenges. To obtain an even wall thickness and reduce the amount of carving, the bowl was turned thin with a number of wide Saturn-like rings from which to retain the spikes. After the bulk of the rings was carved away and the spikes blocked out, came the tricky task of reducing the wall to an even thickness while ensuring that the curve of the profile remained as flowing as possible from every angle. Oudet sanded the carved surface to fair the curves on the profile, and finally hammered it to contrast with the smoother spikes. This bowl can be displayed in a number of positions, so it becomes a little interactive sculpture.

▲ "Endeavour To Persevere," by Art Liestman big leaf maple, 3 7/8 in. by 2 in. (95mm × 50mm). The title can be read in the pierced dancing figures using a code from Arthur Conan Doyle.

▼ Vaughn Richmond drilled the holes in this 9-in. by 2¾-in. (230mm × 70mm) jacaranda bowl, then shaped them using a jeweller's three-corner file.

Piercing

If you like the challenge of making thin bowls and want to display how thin and uniform your wall thickness is, piercing is a great way to show off your skill. But don't forget the sculptural possibilities that holes in thicker walls present, like those in Neil Scobie's Huon pine bowl pictured at the bottom of page 148.

Cutting into a thin bowl wall is not for the faint-hearted, because one slip can easily provide an unwanted design opportunity. End grain is particularly weak structurally, and you need to be careful not to snap off corners, especially when filing or sanding filigree or working around sharp points. High-speed drills, used carefully, stress the wood least as you carve.

To ensure that a frieze-like pattern, such as the figures capering around Art Liestman's "Endeavour To Persevere," photo at left, doesn't wander all over the place, mark a pair of lines within which to lay them out. Do this while

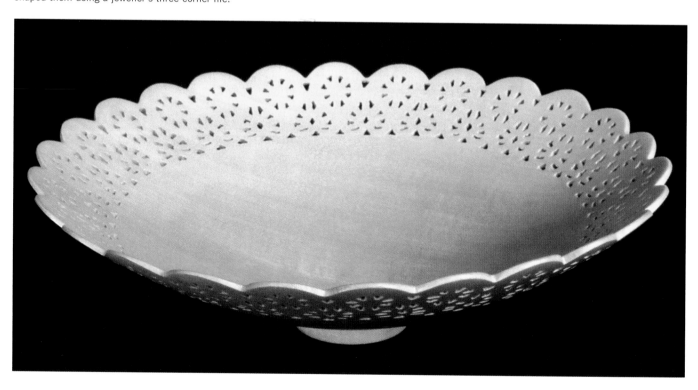

the bowl is still on the lathe using a 2B or 3B pencil. The lines and any other layout marks in such a soft pencil are easy to sand away with fine abrasive once the piercing is done.

The triangular holes that decorate the rim of Vaughn Richmond's 9-in. by 2¾-in. (230mm × 70mm) jacaranda bowl, photo at the bottom of the facing page, were first drilled, then shaped using a triangular jeweller's file. After that, they were sanded using narrow strips of 600-grit abrasive. It sounds like some form of therapy, but Richmond observes that it's the sort of job you keep for watching an Ashes Test Match (five-day cricket matches between England and Australia).

An irregular pattern, like the lattice carved by Gordon Pembridge in the rim of his large bowl, photo below, can absorb the occasional wandering cut, whereas a missing frond or leaf on a more regular or structured design, like his "Fern Bowl," photo at right, is likely to detract from the overall effect. Random patterns are a good way to start.

▲▼ Graphic designs, like these from Gordon Pembridge, look best pierced through an even wall thickness. The 7⅛-in.- (180mm) diameter "Fern Vessel," above, made from New Zealand totara, is stained black with gold leaf and a lacquer spray finish. The bowl below is swamp kauri, 12⅝ in. by 2 in. (320mm × 50mm).

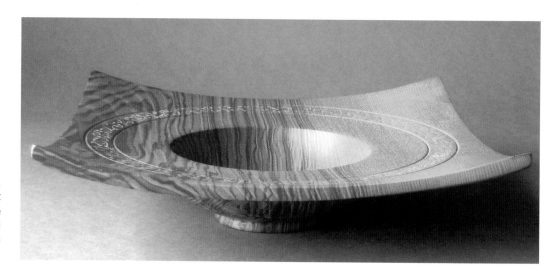

▲ For this formal design, Benoît Averly ensured that the turned bowl and frieze are perfectly centered within the 8-in. (200mm) square of olive ash.

Squaring Up

When bowl turners begin finding rounded forms monotonous, they often turn to the technical challenges of square-edged pieces, like the olive ash bowl turned by Benoît Averly, photo above, and then to more dramatic shapes, as in the photos through the rest of this chapter. Square bowls like Averly's look best if the rim is uniformly thick or tapered evenly to the corners.

To turn square-edge blanks safely, without the corners slicing your fingers or catching and breaking off, set the square blank into a disk for turning. To do this, glue a waste block to each edge, find the center on the blank, and bandsaw a disk on that center. After turning the bowl and cutting off the waste blocks,

▼ The product of a decorating workshop, the carving on these not very good bowls has tremendous energy.

Benoît Averly's signature bowls are designed also to stand on end as sculptures. The rectangular elm form, 5¾ in. by 13¾ in. (145mm × 350mm), sits flat on the table, whereas the 12⅝-in. (320mm) walnut square stands on three small black feet that mirror the buttons on top.

clean up each edge on a belt sander or disk sander, or use a plane. If the sides are sanded at right angles to the bowl's base, from above the bowl will look square. If the bowl is tilted off its base at an angle for sanding, you will remove the stand-up corners, and although the edge is flat in one plane, from above it looks curved, like the blue bowl, right, in the photo at the bottom of the facing page. It's worth sacrificing a few less-than-satisfactory round bowls to see what happens when you cut the rim away from round. Always lay the bowl on its side or upside down on its rim so there is no space between the point where the blade enters the wood and the saw table.

The colored bowls in this photo are products of a "Beyond The Bowl" workshop during which students were encouraged to try all manner of hacking, hewing, texturing, and coloring techniques. The blue bowl had particularly dull grain, so it was an ideal candidate for experimenting. The round rim was cut on the bandsaw to make it near square, then sanded on a disk sander tilted up about 35 degrees so the edge is curved when viewed from above, even though flat when viewed from the side. The red bowl is barely an indentation in a very rough rectangular block. The form was made to be heavily incised or otherwise textured. The rims of the long sides do not match because the blank was not cen-

tered properly on the lathe. This could have been rectified but didn't worry anyone at the time in a group bent on experimenting with carving and color. It is fruitful in explorations to favor the journey over the destination.

Benoît Averly's off-center spherical holes set in squared and sculpted blocks of ash, photos above, are horizontal sculptures that can still be used as bowls. They are designed to stand on end as sculptures in their own right when not in use. When turning squares and rectangles, it pays to have them oversize on the lathe so you can saw or carve the edges once the turning is done and the job is no

This 10⅝-in.- (270mm) diameter multi-axis "Four-in-One" was turned by 14-year-old Luke Crowsen under the guidance of Terry Scott. Very accurate mounting is required to ensure that the hollows lie centrally within the circle. The smooth shoulders between the bowls confirm that the curves are smooth.

longer on the lathe. This approach makes it easier to deal with corners that splinter or become rounded during sanding, or for repositioning the hollow and other turned details in relation to the edges.

To produce a symmetrical group of dishes within a disk like the four-in-one form in the photos above and left, you need extremely accurate chucking then very careful layout and turning if the whole is to look well balanced. Luke Crowsen got all this dead right, as we can see by comparing the position of the hollows within the circle. The crisp shoulders between each dish are smooth curves, indicating that each internal curve flows uniformly.

Bowls with Legs

Throughout the Pacific Islands and Sub-Saharan Africa there is a long tradition of carving wooden bowls with legs (which are long) or feet (which are short and stubby). Invariably, these are entirely carved, but of course we turners can get the hollowing—the laborious and tricky part—done a lot faster. The aim, visually, is for the legs to look as though either they could have been attached after the bowl was completed, rather like the spikes in the photo at the top of page 149; or they grew out of the bowl profile like volcanic cones, as in the photo at the bottom left of page 101, or at the bottom of page 106.

The usual approach for turners is to leave a pedestal foot on the bowl, as was the case in the photo below, whose cross-section is that of the feet you'll end up with. Working this way, it is relatively easy to turn curves either side of the pedestal foot that will flow smoothly through the space between the individual feet. See also the photo at the bottom of page 143.

By contrast, the feet that turn into arms that cradle Andrew Potocnik's Tasmanian blackwood bowl, photo at the bottom of this page, require a lot more carving. The deep recess in the base defined the height of the feet. Then saw cuts from the rim to the corner of the recess in the foot defined the legs, making the corner between the buttress and the profile straight. Rather than recreate a turned surface between the legs, Potocnik flattened the facets toward the base to create a far subtler form, transforming the round rim to a near-square base.

▼▼ The feet on these bowls are all that remain of a turned pedestal foot, the rest having been carved away. Made by Neil Scobie, below, and Andrew Potocnik, bottom.

▲ Terry Scott turned the six spines individually, then glued them to the bowl and faired the transitions before staining and lacquering the outside.

Taking a different approach, Terry Scott turned each of the six arms supporting his 6 ¼-in. (160mm) "Horned Bowl" separately, then attached these to the bowl, photo above. To achieve the triangular cross section and then the curve to fit the bowl profile, it was necessary to turn each arm on several axes. On a hemispherical bowl, such arms could be cut from a ring whose internal diameter matches the external diameter of the bowl, but Scott's asymmetric profile makes for a far better form. After cleaning up the joints and

blending the arms into the bowl surface, Scott stained the bowl black and sprayed the outside with about twenty coats of lacquer.

On wider rims you can lift the bowl off the table by attaching legs in a more conventional manner, as on the three variations by Andrew Potocnik in the photos below left and on the facing page. The challenge here is making three or four legs near identical and exactly the same length. This approach allows you to experiment with combinations of woods and even veneered board. The Tasmanian blackwood, rear, and mulberry bowls in the photo below left are each one piece, with a definition line cut where the flat rim meets the bowl, so they look as though they might be separate pieces joined. The legs are fixed with steel pins as well as glue. These are relatively stable woods, so these pieces are unlikely to warp.

For assured stability, Potocnik used veneered MDF for the rims of the bowls in the photos on the facing page. In the one at top, the top of the rim is a bird's-eye maple veneer, while the under surface is covered with gold leaf. Potocnik turned the bowl section separately out of maple, as well as the ebonized ring.

▼ Tasmanian blackwood, 9⅞ in. (250mm) square, and mulberry 5½ in. (140mm) square, by Andrew Potocnik, 1999.

The pseudo Macassar ebony used for the triangular rim in the photo below is New Age Veneer on MDF. The 8⅝-in.- (220mm) diameter Australian mountain ash bowl is separated from the base by three turned and tapered dowels pinned to the bowl. The bowl is removable.

Most woods will warp to some degree with changes in humidity. Think, for example, of wooden doors jamming within their frames in some seasons and not others. Consequently, a bowl of natural wood with four or more feet is likely to rock on two of them at some stage, even if only for a couple of months a year. It is for that reason I prefer to use three feet: they guarantee stability for eternity, even though the bowl might change shape.

▲▼ Andrew Potocnik used veneered MDF for the rims of both these assembled bowls to provide a stable platform for the legs. In the one above, the underside of the 6-in.- (150mm) diameter bowl is finished with gold leaf. The triangular rim, below, stands 4 in. (100mm) high, and the bowl is 8⅝ in. (220mm) in diameter.

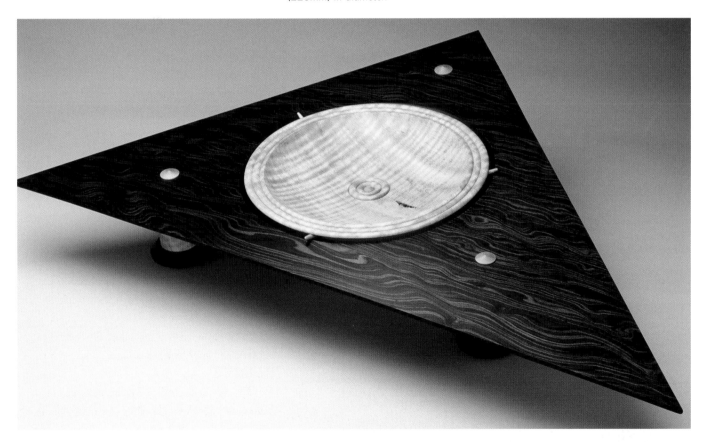

Three feet guarantee stability for eternity.

FURTHER READING

Boase, Tony. *Woodturning Masterclass*. Lewes, East Sussex, UK: Guild of Master Craftsmen Publications, 1995.

———. *Bowl Turning Techniques Masterclass*. Lewes, East Sussex, UK: Guild of Master Craftsmen Publications, 1999.

Darlow, Mike. *Woodturning Design*. Exeter, NSW: The Melaleuca Press, 2003.

———. *Woodturning Techniques*. Exeter, NSW: The Melaleuca Press, 2001.

Hoadley, R. Bruce. *Understanding Wood*. Newtown, CT: The Taunton Press, 2000.

O'Donnell, Liz and Michael. *Decorating Turned Wood*. Lewes, East Sussex, UK: Guild of Master Craftsmen Publications, 2002.

Raffan, Richard. *Taunton's Complete Illustrated Guide to Turning*. Newtown, CT: The Taunton Press, 2005.

———. *Turning Bowls*. Newtown, CT: The Taunton Press, 2002.

———. *Turning Wood*. Newtown, CT: The Taunton Press, 2008.

Wood, Robin. *The Wooden Bowl*. Ammanford, Carmarthenshire, UK: Stobart Davies Ltd., 2005.

PHOTO CREDITS

Unless otherwise noted, photographs and bowls in this book are by Richard Raffan. Following is a list of photo credits for bowls not made by Richard Raffan.

CHAPTER 1
p.13: Bill Luce
p.17: Richard Raffan

CHAPTER 3
p.62, top: Richard Raffan
p.69: Richard Raffan
p.71, top: Richard Raffan

CHAPTER 4
p.91, top: Richard Raffan;
    bottom: Dick Veitch
p.95, center: Dick Veitch
p.96, center and bottom: Dick Veitch
p.97, top: Dick Veitch;
    center: Gordon Pembridge;
    bottom: Richard Raffan

CHAPTER 5
p.102: Bill Luce
p.103: Richard Raffan
p.109: Gordon Pembridge
p.111, center: Richard Raffan

CHAPTER 6
p.114: Richard Raffan
p.116, top: Bill Luce
p.117, bottom: Benoît Averly
p.118, top: Andrew Potocnik;
    bottom: Bill Luce
p.120, top: Richard Raffan
p.121: Andrew Potocnik
p.124, both: Andrew Potocnik
p.125, top left: Richard Raffan;
    top right: Andrew Potocnik;
    center: Tim Skilton;
    bottom: Richard Raffan
p.126, both: Bill Luce
p.128, bottom: Pascal Oudet
p.129, both: Richard Raffan
p.130, top: Richard Raffan;
    bottom: Dick Veitch
p.131, top: Dick Veitch
p.132: Richard Raffan
p.133, center: Andrew Potocnik

CHAPTER 7
p.136: Trevor Hart
p.137: Gordon Pembridge
p.138: Vaughn Richmond
p.139: top: Tony Boase;
    bottom left and bottom right: Richard Raffan

p.140, top: Hayley Smith;
    bottom: Richard Raffan
p.141, both: Richard Raffan
p.142: Richard Raffan
p.143, top: Richard Raffan;
    bottom: Dick Veitch
p.144, top: Liam Flynn;
    bottom left and bottom right: Andrew Potocnik
p.145, both: Dick Veitch
p.146, top: Vaughn Richmond;
    bottom left: Alex Rogysky
p.148, top: Kenji Nagai;
    center and bottom: Neil Scobie
p.149: Pascal Oudet
p.150, top: Kenji Nagai;
    bottom: Alex Rogysky
p.151, both: Gordon Pembridge
p.152, top: Alain Granieri
p.153, both: Alain Granieri
p.154, both: Dick Veitch
p.155, top: Neil Scobie;
    bottom: Andrew Potocnik
p.156, top: Dick Veitch;
    bottom: Andrew Potocnik
p.157, top: Andrew Potocnik;
    bottom: N.T. Photography

INDEX